I0209682

PORCELAIN MOTHS

Books by Joe Ricker

Walkin' After Midnight
Some Awful Cunning
Porcelain Moths
All the Good in Evil (*)
Still Monsters (*)

(*) Coming Soon

JOE RICKER

PORCELAIN MOTHS

DOWN&OUT
BOOKS

Copyright © 2021 by Joe Ricker

All rights reserved. No part of the book may be reproduced in any form or by
any electronic or mechanical means, including information storage and retrieval
systems, without permission in writing from the publisher, except by a reviewer
who may quote brief passages in a review.

Down & Out Books
3959 Van Dyke Road, Suite 265
Lutz, FL 33558
DownAndOutBooks.com

The characters and events in this book are fictitious. Any similarity to real
persons, living or dead, is coincidental and not intended by the author.

Cover design by Joe Ricker and Lance Wright

ISBN: 1-64396-133-0
ISBN-13: 978-1-64396-133-0

PART ONE

ONE

February 17, 1978, 6:43 p.m.

When Maggie Remick stepped from the hospital entrance with her newborn, only the cold was waiting for her. A few steps into her walk home she spotted the abandoned shopping cart by the road. It lay on its side against the snowbank like a distrait pedestrian who had just met the bumper of a speeding mid-sized sedan. The sidewalk was icy, and she feared falling with the baby in her arms. But, mostly, she didn't want to keep it so close to her. Holding it in one arm, she yanked on the wheeled metal cage with her free hand. In just a few seconds, her fingers had gone raw in the cold—the knuckles seized into a brittle claw. The cart broke free when she kicked it. Chunks of ice and snow rattled from the tiny bars. She pulled it to its wheels.

The infant squirmed against the cold metal when she put it in the cart. She moved down the sidewalk, her hands trembling against the handle. The plastic over the top of it was broken off, and the exposed steel bar burned against the first crease of her knuckles. The cart was difficult to push over the packed snow on the sidewalk, but most of the walk was downhill, toward the church at the bottom, then flat for a while until she got to the intersection where the store was. She knew that at the pace she was moving the owner would spot her with his cart and take it from her. He wouldn't care about the baby.

Her baby had been born a few days before at dawn, and she'd fallen asleep as the light snuck through the window and crawled up the side of her hospital bed. She spent those few days relieved that the weight of the child was no longer inside her, and she'd refused to hold the baby until now. The cart should have seemed like a stroke of luck for her, but Maggie wasn't lucky. The baby cried as the cart wobbled. The cry bothered her, and it seemed louder in the cold even with the blanket muffling the noise. Her legs were still a little numb, like the rest of her, and what pain she'd had in the warmth of the hospital was outmatched by the cold chewing away at her fingers, now slicing beneath her nails.

At the edge of the sidewalk the snow wasn't packed down as much and she guided one of the front tires through it to keep her balance, to keep the cart from careening down the hill. She quietly hoped for the passing headlights to warm her hands, but they only shined on the lack of mercy the cold had for her. At the bottom of the hill she paused and waited for cars to stop at the crosswalk before she pushed on, ignoring the hand waving that urged her to move faster over the street, as if the discomfort of the cold had climbed into their cars the way it had into her bones.

The cars crept by, and it made Maggie feel as if her shoes had been tied together like the boys did when she was in grade school, back when they thought she was a charming little doll, and they only wanted to steal a kiss and keep her from chasing them. The cold had her there, in the night, trying to pin her down. Like tires rubbing through the buildup of ice and snow in the wheel wells, Maggie continued. Music came from the cars adjusted a little louder as the vents smothered the passengers with comforting warm air that she knew was there. Metal chiming sang from the chain-link fence as it shook against the posts. The wind bullied a clear piece of plastic against the fence and a corner of it whipped at her, snapping in the air like the bite of a cornered animal.

One of the clerks from the store huddled against the corner of the building, pulling quick drags from his cigarette. He pushed his knees together and tossed his cigarette into the snow piled between the sidewalk and the street. The blinking red light of the intersection pulsed and shined off the patches of ice in the road. Almost there, she whispered—the comfort for her, not the baby. Her lips had gone dry, chapped to the flakiness of burned paper, and above her lip, moisture froze against the edges of her nostrils. She crossed another street and passed the two houses before her mother's. In her last few paces, she looked forward to the kindness the shelter of her mother's house would offer, what the cold and Limington, New York, refused to.

The warmth of the kitchen fell around her. Edith, her mother, sat at the table, a cup of tea gone cold before her. Her curled, arthritic fingers and her palms pressed against the flat surface of the hand-carved mahogany. The woman's eyes narrowed, and she lifted a hand to press the bridge of her glasses higher on her nose with the warped, swollen joint of her index finger. Edith's lips had gone so thin with age, a razor thin line as they pressed together. The pungent smell of hair dye lingered in the air and burned in Maggie's nose. A gold crucifix floated on the white turtleneck Edith wore—daunting, like a knocker on an oversized wooden door begging to be slammed on a house that wouldn't welcome her.

Edith stared at the bundle in her daughter's arms, then stood and left he room. Maggie put the baby on the center of the table and shed her jacket. She sat and pressed her hands between her thighs and tried to still herself from the shiver coiling around her. The baby's arms jerked beneath the blanket and she freed a hand to pull it open. Pictures of Maggie's brother hung in brass frames throughout the kitchen. Where there had been pictures of Maggie, new frames with his image haunted her former space. A motorcycle accident. He'd been drunk. Maggie only ever remembered him drunk. Her half brother, now idolized in the droopy eyed pictures her mother kept on the walls. Maggie looked away from the pictures and clenched her teeth.

The baby squinted in the light of the room, and Maggie let her head sink to the edge of the table. The furnace kicked on in the basement, the rumble of something prehistoric, and Maggie slipped her boots off and pressed her feet into the vibration in the floor. More crying. Maggie lifted her head, her eyelids ready to quit and close for good. She took the baby into the bathroom with her and shut the door. The vent blew warm air against her skin as she stripped over it, casting her clothes into the corner past where the baby lay on the floor.

She sat against the wall with her heels against the tub and rolled her toes over a crack in the porcelain. The baby, red and blotchy, was quiet and naked on the linoleum beside her. His right hand quivered and brushed against her leg. Steam rose around the spouting faucet and cast a veil of fog over the window. Outside, what had started as a tenuous dusting of snow had turned into a white chaotic madness of snowflakes. The night got darker and winter tucked its shoulder into the blizzard and pushed it a little harder. Maggie stared at the window.

For months she'd watched the foliage erupt in the trees outside from where she knelt on her hands and knees at the rim of the toilet each morning. With her growth and unfamiliar discomfort, the hottest parts of the year kept her sticky with sweat through the night. The night eventually took bigger bites of the day until there was barely any left, and she moved through the cold and darkness hunched and pulled down by the weight of what was inside her. Each night she had laid in bed hoping that the growth would diminish and be gone in the morning. She whispered horrible fates that God would not redeem. And when that desire was unanswered by God, she would hope even more for tragedy, even of her own fate, so the ridicule would be gone and the weight of her sin and the weight of the guilt her mother forced on her would be gone, too, but the baby came. It had finally arrived.

The water was too hot as she tested it with the tips of her fingers. She dropped the seat on the toilet and sat, resting her head against the windowsill. The baby, in a continuous spasm and its eyes closed, flexed his mouth. His thin lips curled open and a deep red hole where the tongue worked against his gums let out a choking cough.

After a while, the water had cooled, and she held the baby at the surface. His lips had closed and it was quiet, as if the drops from the faucet cooed the baby into a calm. Maggie's arms ached with the weight of the child—the effort of her support knifed a pain down the sides of her stomach and the weak muscles of her abdomen. She waited for it to open its eyes—iridescent blue and a hint of yellow. Babies could only see shadow, she was told, and she wondered how suddenly those first hints of color would come. The baby sunk below the surface as she withdrew her hands—fingers pruned and pale and thin black lines in the folds. The nameless thing's lips sealed and it lay on the bottom of the tub with a tiny bubble clinging to a nostril—its eyes closed, unable to dream of safety or foresee his fate.

The water was clear, and the baby's fingers worked through it in an attempt to swim or wave goodbye. Maggie lowered her head and relaxed her wrists letting the tips of her fingers sift through the water. There was quiet in her mind, finally, and Maggie let her thoughts slip into a memory of her youth.

When she was a small girl, she'd asked her grandfather once if it were true that he'd drowned a sack of kittens a pond. The old man admitted the crime and gave her knowledge that drowning was like going to sleep. His answer gave her comfort in the fate of the kittens, and Maggie accepted his actions as less brutal than she'd imagined—him holding the sack beneath the surface while the claws of their tiny paws pierced the fabric and left his hands bloody and his ears drenched with gurgled meows.

Another bubble formed on the baby's nostril, the previous having risen to the water's surface. Twenty-three seconds passed and the baby continued to move—soft sloping movements of its limbs, without struggle or panic, until his hand brushed against the tip of Maggie's little finger and latched on.

TWO

Spring 1995

Harley pinched a bubble from his lips and saw it pop at the surface. Maggie and Nick were in the living room completing their afternoon romp. Submerged in the small tub, Harley could feel the vibrations of their movement—the couch thumping against the wall, Maggie's palm slapping the trim of the side window, the steady cadence of his heartbeat as the water went cool.

Harley sat up breaking the smooth flat pane of the water's surface. It rushed off him in song roving against the sides of the tub. He looked at his watch. Two minutes four seconds. He was getting better at holding his breath, allowing his body's panic to drone into a soft electric hum. Nick grunted his last few thrusts into Maggie, and Harley reached over his head to the towel hanging behind him and pulled it down over his face. He stood, sending the water into another furious displacement, and stepped from the tub.

He patted himself dry with the towel, a rag fringed on all sides and stained with the things it had soaked up from the floor and in laundry baskets. Nick pounded his way to the bathroom and Harley wrapped himself in the thin towel, water still dripping from his hair. He met Nick at the door. His mother's lover stood there with a cigarette dangling loosely from his bite, the same manner in which the man's jeans hung on his narrow hips, the fly

7

open, and the button only mostly fitted through its hole. His elbows were grids of a spiderweb tattoos, letters crossed each of his knuckles too faded to determine, warnings of mercy and death wrapped around his arms like black veins. Harley pushed closer to the door giving Nick room to pass so he could exit.

"What kind of a teenage boy takes a bath?" Nick asked.

Harley squeezed the twist in the towel and shrugged. He slipped sideways between the door and Nick's shoulder. Maggie sat on the couch buttoning her shirt and Harley passed her on his way to his room. Neither of them exchanged a glance. The sound of Nick pissing followed Harley through the apartment.

Harley pulled his pants on and sat at the edge of his bed. He took the snow globe from the windowsill and shook it. Inside, a small two-story house—the kind clichéd with happy, perfect families who ate dinner together and had family night by the fireplace—was the only thing unmoving. The white specks eddied inside the sphere after he put it down. Eventually, those specks settled. They always settled. The chaos inside the globe would eventually end, regardless of how violently it was shaken.

A calico cat lurked beneath the bush outside his bedroom window. Trash bags were set out on the sidewalk for the next morning's pickup, pizza boxes stacked next to them like winos sleeping off the headache. A group of kids Harley knew from school shuffled to a car with swim trunks and towels and coolers on their way to Sylvan Beach or Ithaca, somewhere Harley was never taken or invited to, all of them going somewhere, passing his window as if it didn't exist—an empty shell placed on the landscape of their world. Harley rolled to his back and traced the cracks in the ceiling through the paint like a map he was trying to memorize—a journey that led only to the empty corners of his world. The smell of Maggie's cigarette wafted into the room and the sound of Nick's shower hissed through the apartment. Harley closed his eyes and imagined the burn of sand on his feet, the tightening of his skin from a day in the sun, waves curling around his ankles. His door burst open.

Nick stood there, water dripping from him and wetting patches in his jeans. "Think you could have saved some fucking hot water?"

Harley sat up. "Save? Like in a bucket?"

"You know how fucking cold the water is? And there's not even a towel to dry off with."

"You used two of them yesterday to clean your motorcycle. Maybe you should have only used one."

"That mouth of yours is going to get you in a lot of trouble."

"My mouth didn't use the towels to clean off that hunk of shit that won't even run."

Nick gritted his teeth. "Okay, Harley. Keep it up."

"Whatever, Nick."

Nick stared down at Harley, a slight side to side movement in his jaw worked like the gentle, persistent rub against a stain. Harley leaned to his side putting his back to Nick and looked out the window.

Maggie and Nick went out onto the front porch, each with a beer. Nick sat on the railing and drank, quickly tossing the empties he crushed in his hands onto the lawn or in the bushes just below Harley's window. Their voices were muffled beyond the glass, but Harley could still hear them.

"Fucking kid's got an attitude problem, Maggie."

"Just leave him alone, Nick." Maggie dropped her cigarette butt to the porch step and toed it out. "He's not hurting anyone."

Nick popped open another beer. "He's a fucking weirdo. He doesn't have any friends. All he does is sit in the tub or in his room and play with that fucking snow globe. He's probably a faggot."

"I have to go," Maggie said. She stood and kissed Nick's cheek.

"Thanks for leaving me here with your pickle-kissing son."

"I'll be back in a few hours."

"I'm gonna need some beer. And cigarettes."

Maggie stepped off the porch and walked down the sidewalk. Nick pushed himself from the railing and downed his beer. He turned and looked into Harley's window, then made his way through the house. Harley tried his best to ignore the clanging and movement in the kitchen. Nick went outside and Harley listened to the hard spray of water into the plastic bucket Nick used to wash his motorcycle parts. Footsteps charged through the apartment, a heavy thumping against plastic. Harley sat up. Nick hefted the bucket and slammed the water down on Harley. Cold tightened everything in him, even his bones. The ice cubes in the bucket came out in a solid chunk. The sharp edges of ice block raked down Harley's face, the weight of it busting his lip and nose and a thin line of blood warmed a path over his chin through the water.

"Not so fucking smart now, are you?"

Harley shivered and rolled his face into the drenched mattress. Nick moved back through the house hitting the doorframes with the empty bucket as Harley tried to catch his breath.

Harley sat at the edge of his bed shivering while Nick ate his dinner. He sat there as Nick drank more beer, a pile of crushed aluminum growing beside the couch. He sat there while the sun moved toward setting and burned red and orange behind the clouds. When Nick went to piss, Harley came from his room and slipped Nick's Zippo from the TV tray into his pocket. He snuck past the bathroom doorway and outside. The towels Nick had used for cleaning lay over the seat of his motorcycle, the black gas tank glistening even in the dying light of the day. Harley removed the gas cap and stuffed the towel into the hole. He emptied the half-used quart of oil over the leather seat, the saddle bags, and the handlebars. The flame of the Zippo lapped at the air and Harley felt his heartbeat quicken. Deeper, sinking through his guts, he felt a swirl of heat move through his groin as he put a flame to the edge of the rag. The expulsion of light and heat forced him to stagger back, and he caught himself against the maple at the edge of the yard. Fire surged from the bike and Harley leaned against the tree, pressing his face into the bark. The blaze shimmered in the mineral fragments of the gravel driveway. Harley pushed his hand into his pocket and felt how hard he was in his pants.

Nick burst from the apartment, his arms flailing like a boxed primate, silhouette blurred by the black smoke. The fire rose and Harley wanted to swallow the beauty of it, capture it and hold it somewhere, make it his captive. Nick stopped moving when he looked in Harley's direction, his hands flashing into fists, and he circled the fire toward Harley. Harley ran, reluctant to leave the flames, through the backyard. He hopped the fence into the neighbors' garden, looking over his shoulder at the fire, ignoring Nick, until he rounded the corner of the neighbors' house, and there were no distracting flames. Nick panted from the middle of the street, making gasping attempts to yell for Harley, but he couldn't catch him, and wouldn't.

Harley backtracked and cut across the yards between Union and North Street. He ran down the train tracks, his ankles straining against the unevenness of the ties and rocks scattered between them. He ran past the backs of tin-sided warehouses and past the rusted, graffitied rail cars where two sections of track intersected until he hit Watson Street. He trotted down Watson toward the bridge and Interstate 81. In his mind he thought he'd stand at the north ramp for 81 and hitch a ride up to Syracuse, but when he got to the bridge over the East River, he stopped, realizing he'd have nothing to do when he got there except try to find a way back.

The bridge was green steel, rusted in patches like knuckle scabs breaking with the flex of a fist. Halfway across, he turned to look down the river. Cars rushed by pulling into the gas station or the Army Navy store across the street. The water below him was clear, but brown gunk clung to the rocks on the riverbed. The water treatment plant was to the right, and Harley wondered how sick he would get if he drank the water. Harley climbed the rail and sat on top of it, wedging his feet into the square rungs. The tree branches on the side of the river dipped into the water and Harley slouched and rubbed the singed hairs from the backs of his hands.

His throat burned from the run there. His jaw hung as he gulped air through his mouth. Saliva was thick around his gums and his teeth ached. Harley slipped his hand under his shirt and felt the coolness of his skin, the metronome thump of his heart. Blood had dried in clumps inside his nose, and he fingered them from his nostrils as he tried to slow his breathing. Mosquitos buzzed in his ears and he let them take his blood without even the wave of his hand to shoo them off. Instead, he ground down the flint on Nick's Zippo.

Police lights flashed in his peripheral vision, growing brighter until the cruiser stopped. He wanted to look over at them to see if their guns had been drawn. He waited to hear Nick's screaming, but it didn't come. An officer approached him slowly.

"Son, you want to swing 'round and step onto the sidewalk?" he asked.

Harley righted himself and gripped the round pole he sat on. He unhitched his feet from the rungs and swung his legs over the rail and dropped to the sidewalk.

"Your name Harley Remick?" the cop asked.

Harley put his thumbs in his pockets and nodded.

"I'm going to need you to turn around and put your hands behind your head."

THREE

Maggie sat on the other side of the glass with her arms crossed. A few minutes later Harley emerged from a steel door with a corrections officer. He looked small, like he had when he was a boy, in the orange scrubs issued by the county jail; a clubhouse for the petty criminals and the homeless in winter who committed menial crimes to get food and shelter. Maggie picked up the phone when Harley sat and he followed suit. His eyes were wrapped in bruises, cartoonish. Maggie looked at his chest, avoiding the darkness on his face.

"I had a good thing, Harley, and you screwed it up."

"You have low expectations, Maggie, if Nick was a good thing."

"He paid part of the rent."

"Try lighting a fire. They're giving me a free place to stay."

"Always the smartass, Harley. Good luck with that mouth of yours in here."

"I don't see why you're so mad, Maggie. One good thing came out of this."

"Good? Something good came out of this?" She looked at his eyes then, seeing that the skin around them was more purple than black. "Please, tell me what is so fucking good about what happened?"

"You finally got rid of me."

Maggie's look of disdain melted down her face, and it

13

seemed, the words were a circular movement of liquid. The words coming from Harley, to Maggie's ear, and her expression swirling into a vortex and emptying from her as Harley stood, hung up the receiver, and walked away.

After the first day or two, Harley embraced the routine of jail. The guards left him alone. Most of them were overweight, and Harley decided that they didn't fuck with him only out of laziness. They had a confident lean on their authority, and they didn't waste their time on anyone who wasn't a threat to that. Harley walked in circles most of the day, around the six steel tables bolted to the floor of the cell block, and nobody stepped in front of him to call him a *fag* or a *loser* the way they did when he walked through the hallways of his high school, or the way Nick had done whenever Harley met him at a doorway. The other inmates left him alone, too, but they reminded him of the men he'd known his whole life, the type of men his mother brought home to fuck her. At one point in his life, he'd hoped that his mother would bring a man home so he could have a father or a friend, but that was never the case. Maggie could not have cared less about a father for him, and the days that she was happiest were the days a check came from the state. Those were the days that he'd hoped for a new bike or shoes or a baseball mitt—days he'd hoped she'd bring him somewhere like the beach or an amusement park or an animal farm. But Maggie would use the money at a bar or loan it to Nick for leather jackets or chrome parts for his motorcycle. Those were the days that taught him the most, the hardest lessons of his life, how not to cry even when it was impossible not to.

After two weeks of pacing, Harley was transferred to a youth facility a few hours north of Limington. He was brought out of the cell block, shackled, and escorted to a van. The seats were soft, and Harley didn't waste time finding sleep. Before the van pulled through the gates, he'd already fallen into the deep, rhythmic breath of sleep. He slept for an hour, until the guards pulled the van into a parking lot and stopped. Harley lifted his head and blinked to adjust his eyes.

Porter, the jail guard who rode in the passenger seat, turned to Harley. "You want anything to eat?" He pointed through the windshield at the McDonald's they had stopped in front of.

Harley squeezed the immediate rumble from his stomach and shook his head. He bowed to scratch an itch on his eyebrow, the shackles forcing him to strain his neck to reach. Porter kept a gaze over Harley for a moment then stepped from the van.

"Look, man," Porter said through passenger door window. "I was friends with your mom's older brother in high school. I also know how much of a fucking piece of shit Nick Kraft is. I doubt you got those black eyes you came in with after you started that fire. The food at North Falls is a step above trash, so this might be the last time you get something worth eating for a while. You want a couple cheeseburgers?"

Harley nodded. Porter had a kind face, one of those faces always drawn to a smile, the eyes unchanged by facial expressions. He had a way of talking to dangerous men that calmed them, obscured their aggressiveness, and Harley was awed by it—something so completely opposite of himself.

Porter returned to the van with the sack of food and a carry tray for drinks. Harley felt an uneasiness seeing that there were three drinks in the tray. Porter climbed into the van, smiling the way he always did, his teeth white, luminous, actually. He handed the driver his food, placed his own on the console, and reached in to hand Harley the food he had gotten him.

"You're not in a hurry, are you?" the driver said to Harley with a mouthful of Big Mac.

His eyes welled. Harley tightened his jaw and looked down on the food. He shook his head, staring at the yellow paper wrapped around the burgers. The warmth that came from them made his palms sweat. Porter reached back and took Harley's wrist. He dangled a set of keys from his finger.

"Not too easy to enjoy this being shackled like you are."

Harley's hand came free from the cuff, and with it a breath of air. It hadn't been until then that he realized how much he'd been holding his breath. He felt his face pinching, the tears heavy enough to pull his head forward as he tried to fight their coming. They ran, despite his hardest effort to fight them, and dropped onto the yellow paper wrapped neatly around something he'd never eaten resting in the palms of his hands.

Porter grabbed the fries from the bag and the drink he'd gotten Harley. He turned to hand them to him, his smile gone. "It's okay, Harley. Take your time. Eat while it's still hot, though." And his smile returned.

"Heya, Remick," the driver said with fries dangling from the corner of his mouth. "If you try to escape, I *will* shoot you in the face."

Harley gave him a stern look then moved his hands from beneath the burgers and smeared the tears from his face with the heels of his hands. He took a long look at Porter and took the fries and the drink.

"Thank you," Harley said.

The driver strained to turn in his seat and look back at Harley. Porter nodded and turned to eat his own food. The three of them sat in the van in the parking lot eating slowly. Harley took small bites. He savored the smell of deep-fry and warm tang of the mustard, the soft texture of food in his mouth, the snap of minced onions, the crispness of the soda, and the taste of the salt from his tears.

There were two staff members who met Harley at the boys' home. They were dressed in black military pants and blue T-shirts that had STAFF in gold letters printed on the back. Their utility belts held a pouch for rubber gloves, a flashlight, radio, and pepper spray. They had crew cuts and soft, doughy faces. The room was bright. A line of fluorescent lights ran down the center of the narrow room. The walls were a dingy yellow, but the smell of fresh paint lingered in the air. There was a folding table centered before Harley. A pile of clothes and sheets were folded and stacked neatly in one corner. The guards from the jail and the staff at the home exchanged their paperwork for Harley.

"So you like to start fires, eh?" A staff member stood in front of Harley tapping his pen against the clipboard with Harley's transfer papers on them. His hands were small and he had short, big knuckled fingers. He was pale, and like the rest of him, his face was bland, soft, like handwriting that is neither scratchy nor elegant—something legible, and it was easy for Harley to see that the hardest challenge of the man's life would be him.

Harley shook his head.

"There are four ways to answer questions here, Remick. Do you know what they are?"

Harley shook his head again.

"Yes, sir; No, sir, Yes, ma'am; No, ma'am. Two of these responses are appropriate for the question I just asked you. Do you need me to repeat the question?"

Harley shook his head.

"Smartass, hunh?"

"Harley's one of those quiet inmates. The kind we like," Porter said.

"Well, things are a little different here at NFHB. And here, we don't like boys who can't answer questions or show respect for authority." He lifted his ID card that dangled on a lanyard around his neck. He tapped on his name in bold, black print. "McMillan," he said. "I'll be taking a special interest in you, Harley—David—Remick."

Porter took the paperwork. Another staff member handed Harley a pair of dark blue Dickies pants and a T-shirt. They'd been used. Harley took in the thrift store scent of them—cheap detergent and the mustiness of storage.

"If you need socks or underwear or a pillow, you'll have to set up an account with the commissary," the man said. He handed Harley a plastic bag. "Step into the bathroom over there and get changed so we can return your scrubs to the CO's."

"Three minutes," McMillan stated.

Harley tongued food from his teeth as he stripped the orange and pulled the pants over his legs. He slid into the T-shirt and folded the pants then counted to twenty after McMillan called out that there was only thirty seconds left. The door had remained open, and Harley simply stared at him in the mirror. Just as McMillan looked up from his watch, Harley exited the bathroom and handed the county clothes over to Porter.

"Take care of yourself in here." He tapped Harley on the shoulder with the clipboard as he followed his partner out.

McMillan put a firm grip on Harley's right tricep and guided him to a door at the far end of the room. He spoke while they walked. "Typically, it's customary to make the newbies feel comfortable when they first arrive. It is a bit of an adjustment, you know, being a piece of shit then getting sent to a place that conforms your behavior. Discipline is a crucial part of how we maintain this place."

The other staff member, who had followed quietly, stepped beside McMillan as they stopped before the doors at the end of the hallway they had just walked down.

"This is your first lesson in discipline, Remick." McMillan lifted his arm and shot a thin, forceful jet of liquid across the bridge of Harley's nose. It burned immediately and Harley's arms tensed. His nose ran. A bursting force of air shot through his mouth when McMillan punched him in the stomach. Harley gasped and felt his legs weaken. He went down, spilling his sheets to the floor. Harley tried to relieve the burning in his eyes, pressing his nose and lips into the floor. The taste of wax and grit entered his mouth, and he felt the thin line between the squares of the flooring against his cheek. He smelled the worn leather of their boots. If he'd been able to cry out, he wouldn't have. When he caught his breath again, he grinned. This was the worst they could do to him.

FOUR

Spring 1997

Maggie stepped through the automatic doors of the small grocery where she worked and met the gloom of the cloudy day with appreciation. She'd gone to Sebastian's the night before and the rum and Cokes she'd drank made her workday an echoing pulse of agony. Conversations through the aisles and the beeping from the scanner at her register bore into her ears like a persistent, spinning router tearing at wood. When the cash drawer would open and clang the ache pushed through her teeth. She was thankful there was no sun to pierce her vision and create more pressure inside her head.

The bench she sat on led to the apartments above the store. Wind rolled through the parking lot and she slipped a button loose to feel it cool the clamminess of her chest. She lit a cigarette and leaned forward, allowing her head to hang. The taste of the cigarette was bitter, but she continued to smoke it. After a few drags, she sat back and looked through the parking lot. A boy, lanky and moving with a vibrant pace, paused when he noticed her looking at him. A smile crept across his face and he moved toward her.

"Can I get a smoke?" he asked.

She picked up the pack of smokes and the lighter and handed them to him. He fumbled to pull a cigarette out, and Maggie admired the olive tint of the skin on his arms and neck and the youth in his face. His eyes paused at her breasts for an extra second as he scanned her. A twitch in his eye warned her of his interests.

"I'm Sean," he said, lighting the cigarette.

He held the lighter out for her to grab. She let him grip and hold onto her two fingers for a moment as she slipped the lighter from his palm. "Uh, hunh," she replied.

Maggie bit her bottom lip and studied him. She forgot about the dulling ache in her head. He was young, not as young as she expected, but she knew what he wanted before he asked for a cigarette. There were always young men looking at her, wanting her to be the older woman that would teach them how to fuck their girlfriends. The woman they would bring their friends to the grocery store to show and tell them how she'd sucked them off in the back seat of their parents' car. That was one thing that didn't change with men even when they aged. They all wanted to be inside her. The only thing stopping a lot of them was her permission. She'd given up on them, their false charms and placebo words. They were the men she enjoyed sex with the most, that she kept around or lived with. The others simply quieted her cravings for a short time. Sex was the thing her body whined for incessantly as if her lack of discernment somehow gave her control, a yearning for a past instance that gave her a predatory outlook on the act. She preferred younger men simply because of their pride. They would kill themselves to keep up with her when her cravings were insatiable, which they often were. She'd never quite been able to make up for her first time.

"So how long have you worked here at the ah—"

"Save it, kid. I have twenty minutes of my break left and I don't plan to waste it waiting for you to get to the point."

"I don't know what you mean."

"Now I have nineteen minutes. You want to take me out or do you just want to fuck?"

"What? Uh."

"You scared?"

He squinted at her. "I ain't scared."

"Good. I get off at eight o'clock."

"Ah, yeah. Okay. I'll see you—"

Maggie stood and walked back into the store.

The next day Maggie's hangover was gone and she was at work wiping the spray cleaner off the conveyer belt. She'd had a particularly slow day, the usual two- or three-item shoppers who'd come in for eggs or milk or a can of baby formula. Halfway through her shift, roughly the time that Sean had visited the day before, Maggie noticed him approaching the store. He'd dressed in a pair of khaki pants and a white polo shirt. His hair was slick with gel, a look that Maggie loathed, and he'd done his best to shave, putting more nicks on his face than he had hair. She muttered to herself and turned to face the register, putting her back to the door. She watched him over her shoulder. He paced the aisles looking at almost every can or package but didn't pick anything up. Darlene, the cashier at the next register, snapped her fingers at Maggie.

"These little fuckers think they can dress up halfway decent and we won't suspect them of stealing anything. Un-fucking-believable." Darlene picked up the phone by her register. "I'm calling the cops."

Maggie shook her head. "Don't do that, Darlene. I'll go talk to him."

"Management has a strict policy on employees confronting shoplifters. The last time that happened, Paul got stabbed. Remember?"

Maggie nodded. "I remember. I sort of know this guy, though. I don't think he's here to steal anything."

Darlene crossed her arms and squinted at Maggie. "He a friend of your son's or something?" She pushed a snotty, sarcastic smirk between her cheeks.

"My son doesn't have any friends. I know what you're thinking, too. For the record, Harley started a fire. He doesn't steal. What is it that your son and boyfriend got caught doing? Selling pot to high school kids, was it?"

Darlene's face went pale, lost the dark blush that typically covered it. Maggie moved down the aisle toward Sean. He placed the can of cranberry sauce he'd been holding back on the shelf. When she got closer, Maggie could smell his cologne.

"Can I help you with something?" Maggie asked. She stood before him with her limbs tucked close to her body. Her hands were clasped behind her back. Even the smile on her face was fake and tense.

"Nah. I'm just looking around." Sean's confident approach toward her yesterday had been lost somewhere. Maggie tilted her head, wondering if his performance had humbled his arrogant adolescent attitude.

"It's a grocery store. Nobody just looks around in a grocery store."

He shrugged. "Okay. I came to see you."

"I don't do repeat performances kid."

Sean's face flushed. "I'm sorry about that. I'm sorry that I lied to you. I just—"

"Save it, okay. You're a kid. I'm twice your age. I was really hungover yesterday, probably still a little drunk, and if I had to do it over again, I'd probably just tell you to piss off."

"So I don't even get a chance to redeem myself?"

"Redeem yourself for what? You're not the first guy I've seen do that. You probably won't be the last."

"Okay. Then can I at least go on one more date with you before you blow me off?"

Maggie pushed her fingers through her hair. "Date? Are you serious?" Her tone had dropped to something less hostile and she focused on Sean's eyes which were frantic, like fingers moving across a wall for a doorknob in the dark. "Aren't there girls your age you could be hanging out with?"

"There are plenty of girls my age. None of them will ever be as hot as you, even if they tried really hard."

"Oh, well thanks, I guess. But I don't think it's a good idea. Your parents probably wouldn't be happy about me robbing the cradle."

"I live with my dad and he's only home once a week. He's always out of town on business or to see his girlfriend. He doesn't care what I do."

There was a pitch to his voice, a specific promise of kindness.

"Tomorrow. Five o'clock. Be here to pick me up."

Sean lifted himself on his toes. Maggie expected him to clap his hands, but he clenched them into fists, folded his arms across his chest. As she walked back to her register and through Darlene's glare, she realized nobody had ever been that excited to go on a date with her. She wondered if it were because he anticipated sex or if it was because he didn't know about Harley. She was topped out at her job making as much as she possibly could, and she'd been there since Harley was born. She couldn't remember a day when she'd been happy about tomorrow.

Thirty minutes before Maggie could punch out the next day, Sean pulled into the lot. She'd gotten up a little earlier that morning to pick out clothes for her date but had decided after about fifteen minutes that she wasn't going to go through with it and wore her usual jeans and low-cut shirt. When she saw that he'd arrived early, she felt bad for him. He was pathetic, but it was a trait that soothed her. His effort and inexperience forced the illusion of charm.

He drove them through Limington and set the cruise control at the speed limit when they got onto Highway 13. Maggie found it cute, but in the way that a pet brings its owner dead things.

"So where are we going?" Maggie asked.

"It's a surprise."

"Oooh. I'm not a fan of those, Sean. I don't really know you that well."

Sean's jaw went slack, as if he were finding a word to begin with.

"I'll tell you what. You can bring me wherever you want as long as it's not to one of your friend's house, anywhere your friends are hanging out, or anywhere secluded."

He drove the two of them to Stewart Park in Ithaca. Maggie remembered her father taking her there when she was young. She'd go through a sleeve of bread, breaking it into pieces for the ducks. When Sean parked the car and pulled a bag of cheese doodles from the floorboard of the back seat, her nostalgia made her insides go hot and a liquid glee purged through her like a melting yellow crayon.

Water lapped at the foot of the lake and tears built at the bottom of Maggie's eyelids. At the edge of Cayuga, Sean opened the bag and tossed a handful of the orange puffs to the few ducks in the water. Foam and seaweed wimpled on the rocks. A faint, rotten smell of eggs followed the wind. Sean offered the opening of the bag to Maggie, and Maggie took a handful. She bit into one and chewed it, turning it into a soggy mess that stuck between her teeth. Gulls swarmed and landed around them, hovering off the water and snatching the treat and ascending. Canadian geese watched from a distance. Sean and Maggie went through the bag matching the frenzy of ducks and gulls. Quacking and screeching formed the dialogue while Maggie and Sean remained quiet save for a few giggles by Maggie. They watched like children at the spectacle, and for the first time since before her pregnancy with Harley, Maggie felt a touch of youth.

Sean continued to meet her, take her on obscure dates, and swing through the store to steal glances at her while she worked. His boyishness charmed her, and his youth reminded her of the things she'd lost because of Harley. Sean's touch would graze her skin as if he were petting a small bird, and when he stroked his fingers through her hair, he did it as if her hair was something he wasn't supposed to touch, unlike the other men she'd known who used her hair like reins while they fucked her, wrapping it in their knuckles and gripping her throat. But there was something missing. Maggie found it impossible to develop the feelings she thought she should have for him. There was something about his kindness that she didn't believe. Or trust. She kept that in the back of her mind. Harley would be back in just a couple months. Maggie savored her moments with Sean, and despite her reservations, on his eighteenth birthday, just a few weeks before Harley's release, Sean asked to move in with her. Maggie, hopeful at a new start, a chance to regain some youth, at least a glimmer of it, agreed.

FIVE

Late Spring 1997

The biggest difference between the boys at the home and the men in county jail were that the boys in the home were in a hurry to prove to each other that they were ready for jail. The men in jail, most of them, did their time quietly. The boys refused to do anything they didn't have to. GED classes were mandatory, but nearly half of the boys at North Falls couldn't read past a third-grade level. They'd take the test for a change in routine and spend that time drawing tits or cocks on their exam papers. In jail, the men there kept their motives to themselves. They played cards or read books. They minded their own business. In the two years that Harley spent at the boys' home, a day hadn't passed that he'd wished he'd spent that time in jail, but he'd fallen into the routine—the challenges of other boys, McMillan's continual attempts to embarrass him, and his commitment to silence.

The boys were kept in bays. Each bay was separated by the amount of risk the boys posed. If they were violent or tried to escape, they were secured in the Red Area, where Harley had spent the entire two years of his stay. There were windows caged with metal screens. Two rows of ten steel bunk beds lined each side of the room. The beds were bolted to the floors to keep boys from tipping them on their sides to hang themselves or to keep them from blockading the entrances. There was a fight almost daily, and when Harley was in the bay, he spent his time on his mattress.

On the day of his release, Harley sat on the edge of his bunk with his temple resting against the steel support pole. Sunlight slanted through the room from the top corners of the windows and the slightest movement cast a glow behind his eyelids. At the end of the bay, McMillan spoke with two other boys, Parker and Wells. Their words were muffled in whispers until McMillan told them he'd be back in ten minutes, which Harley knew would be much longer than that. McMillan said that whenever someone was getting out, and he'd leave Parker and Wells to do whatever in that time.

The boys paced around the bay, laughing and swearing and kicking the mattresses from the bunks for a quick laugh. They'd been sent there from Rochester, commonly referred to as "The Rock" among the other boys.. They were tall, and had about a foot on Harley, but they were skinny and their limbs looked proportionally absurd like the straight lined arms of people in children's artwork. Parker had given himself a teardrop tattoo with a sewing needle and thread and ink he'd made with shampoo and melted plastic. Nobody knew why they'd been sent there except the staff. The boys claimed different things: murder, rape, armed robbery. They'd lost their work privilege, and losing that privilege left them in the bay during the steamy hours of summer while the other boys sweat and got tan and drank soda at lunch. Of course, they received other benefits for being McMillan's lackeys. Cigarettes were the best of those benefits. Porn magazines and candy were also offered, but the porn was especially rare. Parker made his way to the window near Harley's bunk.

"Hey, Hushpuppy," Parker said. "You wanna suck my cock before you go? You know, so you can have something to remember this place by."

Harley kept his eyes closed while Wells joined Parker.

"You know he wants to. Weird motherfucker. Bet he can't wait to get down to Ithaca and gobble all kinds of cock and balls."

Parker snickered, and Wells made his way to the opposite end of Harley's bunk and jerked on the steel pole forcing Harley's head to bob into the sunlight and rap against the pole. Harley folded his arms and kept his eyes closed.

"So what about it Hushpuppy, you want to wrap those pretty little lips around my shit or what?"

Harley felt the lethargic motion of his vocal cords come to life. "You going to pick one?" he asked and opened his eyes.

Wells jumped in the air and slapped his thighs. "Motherfucker spoke. Shit."

Parker squinted. "Pick what?"

"You want me to suck your cock or wrap my lips around your shit? Which one? Pick."

"I knew you were a faggot."

"Isn't that why you want me to suck your cock?"

"Fuck you, Hushpuppy."

"Fucking faggot wants to suck a cock. Shit. I'm telling e'erbody," Wells cackled.

"Tell everyone. What do I care? I'm leaving. You two fucking milk duds are going to be here indefinitely. What are you going to do, Wells, sit in the corner and watch?"

"You're fucking looney, man," Parker said.

"What's wrong, Parker? Afraid Wells is going to see how small your dick is?"

"I ain't got no small dick, white boy."

"Then whip it out."

Wells turned his smile into a look of curiosity toward Parker. Parker looked at Wells and down to Harley.

"You're seriously going to suck my cock?"

"Kinda hard to do that with it in your pants."

Parker looked at Wells again. Wells shrugged. "If you do Parker you gotta do me, too."

"Fine."

The boys moved their shaky hands to their pants and loosed their dicks. Harley slid from the bed and squatted on the balls of his feet. He gripped Parker's dick and squeezed.

"Damn, Hushpuppy. That's a fucking grip," Parker moaned.

Harley showed his teeth and sprang from the balls of his feet into a run. Parker swatted at Harley's head, his wrist, holding his pants at his waist with his other hand. Wells trailed a few feet behind Parker, grabbing for his shoulder. Harley ran across the bay toward the last bunk in the row and dove over the bottom bunk, hurling his weight over the mattress. Parker's face and shins smashed into the rails on the bunk and he folded through the space. Harley rolled across the floor and jumped to his feet as Wells charged around the bunk toward him, a long arm drawn back to throw a wide punch. Harley set his lead foot and dropped Wells with a kick to his balls.

McMillan's key scraped into the lock. He entered with a smile on his face, which quickly lost air and went flat. Parker lay motionless over the bottom bunk, a gash on his forehead seeping blood onto the floor. Wells dry-heaved from a fetal position just a few feet from where McMillan stared at Harley. McMillan fished his pepper spray from his belt and charged toward Harley.

"You really are that fucking stupid, aren't you?" Harley asked.

McMillan fumbled the pepper spray from his hand. His eyelids crawled deeper into his skull as if the sound of Harley's voice sent them scurrying to hide. McMillan crouched slowly, tapping around the floor with his fingers for the canister he'd dropped and leaving his eyes perched, unmoving from Harley.

"You look like someone just caught you shitting on the rug. If you're going to spray me, you may as well do it."

McMillan found the spray and gripped it tightly. He stood and made another step toward Harley.

"Going to be really interesting to hear you explain why you

sprayed me, though."

McMillan smirked and looked over at Parker and Wells. "Not really. You got into a fight. That extends your detainment by thirty days."

"Where were you while this was going on?"

"That doesn't matter. Nobody's going to believe you."

"Right. I haven't spoken a word in two years, and you think they're going to believe that I'm going to speak just to lie? That's not even considering how fucking stupid it would be to get into a fight the day I get out of this shithole. And let's just say for a second they do believe I'm lying. Are they really going to believe a couple of thugs from The Rock got beat up by me, and there's not a scratch on me?"

"Well, we can fix that."

"Sure. Then you'd have to explain why you sprayed me and not them. Then, you have to explain how a fight got that violent before you intervened."

"They're going to believe me over you."

"But they won't believe the three of us over you." Harley pointed two fingers at Parker and Wells.

McMillan arched his eyebrows. "They'll back me."

"Not if you're going to keep me here for another thirty days. Hushpuppy won't be quite so hush-hush anymore."

McMillan glanced at the two boys. They looked down at the floor beyond their feet.

"Spray me. Hit me. Do whatever the fuck you want, McDumbfuck. I'll get you fired."

McMillan's expression had faded into a child-like pout. He crammed the pepper spray back into his belt.

He radioed relief so he could bring Harley to the processing room, then turned and approached Parker and Wells. "You two fucking idiots better stop horsing around. I'm not taking you to the infirmary for this. Go to the other end of the bay and clean yourself up." He moved back to Harley. "Let's go, Remick. Strip your bunk."

31

Harley stood and piled his things onto his bunk. Uniforms were the only personal items he'd been allowed. He pulled the corners of the sheets together and slung the load over his shoulder.

Harley gave Parker and Wells a seductive finger wave on his way by. "By *boyths*."

In the processing room, the room that Harley had entered when he'd first arrived, McMillan slammed the steel door and kicked the chair out from the folding table to sit down on. "Your personal effects will be released to you when your escort arrives."

Harley dropped the sheets and uniforms on the folding table. The boys' home had provided Harley with insight. He'd come to realize that he wasn't alone. Even Parker and Wells were victims of some sort of injustice, some behavior inflicted on them that would go unpunished, but the sadder part of all of it, of all that he had come to learn, was McMillan. He belonged to that small, pitiful group of men harnessed to the humiliation they'd experienced their whole life—being small, the snickers of girls at their tiny dicks, their failure to become cops or soldiers, reasons to take out their inconsolable hypocrisy on boys that reminded them of how big a fucking loser they were—boys who were considered losers themselves. They were chained to their pepper spray and that place. The only place they could find value in their lives was at the boys' home, where they bullied because that was the only place they had control. When they went home and looked in the mirror, the only thing that validated them was the abuse they inflicted on others. Harley shook his head.

McMillan folded his arms over his stomach. "What the fuck is it now, Remick?"

"I don't think I have anything else to say to you."

McMillan slipped his thumbs into his pockets and made the slow approach toward Harley. "There is one last thing I want to give you, Remick, before you leave. A little piece of advice that might help you stay out of this place."

Harley tensed his stomach muscles.

SIX

Maggie counted the three stories of the boys' home as she drove the road leading to it. It looked less like a prison than she'd imagined. As she made that observation, she realized that the last time she'd spoken to Harley, through the chicken-wire glass of the county jail two years before, seemed no longer than a breath. She wondered if she should feel guilty about that, not visiting, but the facility was more than an hour from Limington, and Harley had never asked to see her. The only correspondence she'd received was an official letter from Harley's caseworker stating Harley's release date and that he would need someone to pick him up from the campus. She pulled her car to a stop in a space near the entrance marked VISITOR.

Close to the building, she could see that there were bars on the outside of the windows. Behind them, on the third floor, a group of boys looked down at her. She gathered the change of clothes they'd asked her to bring for Harley, a pair of jeans and a white T-shirt left over from Nick. When she got out of the car she heard the muffled alert for the other boys to join them. Pounding erupted against metal, the steel mesh on the inside of the windows. A chant formed with the cadence of the pounding: *Show us your tits, show us your tits, show us your tits...* The chanting and pounding faded as she ducked into the lobby.

A fat man sat at a desk just inside the entryway. His initial glance in Maggie's direction seemed indifferent as he poked into his gums with a forefinger. After she slid her sunglasses off and approached him, he jumped from his seat and worked his T-shirt around his large belly and into his beltline. His fly was unzipped, and there were yellow mustard stains on the thighs of his black pants. He pawed at the thinning hair on his scalp, flattening it toward his forehead.

"I'm here for my son," she said, removing her sunglasses.

"His name, ma'am?"

"Harley Remick. They told me to bring these." She handed over a plastic grocery bag with a change of clothes.

The man took them and fumbled over the desk for his clipboard, finally taking his eyes from Maggie to find it. He turned a page over and pressed the edge of the clipboard against his stomach, a slot forming in the soft mound of flesh. Maggie slipped a piece of gum from her purse and looked around. Thick wooden doors with frosted glass panes broke the flat, monotonous length of the corridor beyond the guard. Small square tiles lined the walls, teal with a single row of white above them. Specks of black rested in the grout, perhaps what remained of quick graffiti the guard had failed to stop. Maggie reached across her chest to adjust the straps of her purse on her shoulder when she saw the guard staring at her tits over the clipboard.

"The last name is spelled R-E-M-I-C-K." She raised her eyebrows. The guard nodded and went back to scanning.

"Here we go. Remick, Harley-David. Interesting name, Harley-David. Hope he likes motorcycles."

Maggie frowned. "Where do I go from here?"

"Ah, yes. Just head down this hallway." He pointed. "And it's the third door on your left. Dr. Williams's office."

"Thank you."

Maggie started down the hall. Over her own footsteps, she heard the guard move into the hallway, and she clenched her ass and tried not to walk too fast. The lighting was weak fluorescent, copper doorknobs tarnished like forgotten jewelry, and the echo of each step seemed endless as she moved just that short distance with the fat man's leer lurking just over her shoulder. She stopped to knock.

"Just go right in," the guard instructed.

Compared to the hallway, the light in Dr. Williams's office was nearly blinding. She squinted at the secretary and scanned the office. Pale white walls. Deep green carpet. Artificial plants in the back corners. A cardboard box taped shut with Harley's full name across the top sat on the center of the bench against the far wall. *Remick* written on two sides. The secretary was an older woman, her body lumped and squat from years of sitting in spinning chairs. She wore plastic, pink-framed glasses and a lavender skirt suit.

"Can I help you?" She asked.

"I'm here for Harley Remick."

"Oh, yes. And you are?"

"Margaret—Maggie Remick."

"Ms. Remick. I'll let Dr. Williams know you're here."

The woman removed her glasses and moved from her desk. The sheen of her lavender suit made it look wet in the brightness of the room. The gentle knock on the door to her left was less perceptible than the secretary's whispering through the small opening she'd allowed. Dr. Williams shuffled around his office. Williams was tall and had less than an inch of clearance through his office door. A few strands of his disheveled hair reached for the metal trim around the door frame.

"Ms. Remick," Dr. Williams greeted her. "Come in."

The woman tilted her head as Maggie moved past her. Williams pointed his open hand at the two chairs across from her desk. "Have a seat."

Maggie sat and crossed her legs. She secured her purse on her thigh and waited for Williams. He opened a manila folder on his desk and made a ticking sound with his mouth.

"Well, Ms. Is it Misses?"

"Maggie's fine."

"Alright, Maggie. I've been working with Harley since he

came to us and it has been an interesting case. There are some things that we should discuss about his release."

Working? Came to us? The language he used immediately bothered her. Harley didn't go to them. He was sent to them. *Working?* What he meant was observing, prodding, and poking. Tinkering around inside Harley's brain trying to figure out what made him tick. Harley wasn't an interesting case. Harley was a smartass who pissed everyone off. Harley was sent to them for setting a fire.

"Did Harley get his GED?"

"Yes. He's had that under his belt for over a year now. What I wanted to talk to you about are Harley's social skills. See he's what we would classify as—"

"Are you telling me that Harley can't leave?"

"No. Not at all."

"Dr. Williams, I'm sure that there is a lot about Harley that we could talk about, but I had to take off work to come here today, and I need to get back as soon as I can. I don't understand any of this psychology stuff so it might be better if you have some brochures or pamphlets I can give to Harley."

"Oh. I understand. Let me be brief then. Harley hasn't spoken a word in two years." Dr. Williams leaned back in his seat and held his chin.

Maggie's head slumped forward. "What?"

"Absolute silence. It's quite remarkable, actually."

"Remarkable? Harley hasn't spoken in two years?"

"Not a single peep. Not to me or any member of the staff that I'm aware of."

Maggie leaned back and tried to imagine if there had been a time that Harley was quiet. Her memory shuffled through things and set off memories of anger, but even in those, it was never anything he'd said.

Dr. Williams leaned forward and rested his elbows on his desk. "Harley's intent, I believe, when he started that fire was to gain attention. In Harley's case, like many with anti-social disorders such as Harley's, their lashing out is a cry for attention. They've learned to cultivate this behavior to manipulate others. I do have a few questions, though. Did Harley have accidents at night after the age of five?"

"Accidents?"

"Wetting the bed."

"Oh. Yes, actually. I think up until the time he was around eight or ten, maybe twelve."

"You can't be more specific?"

"No. I don't really remember when Harley stopped wetting the bed. It's not something I was very happy about."

"Hmmm. Was Harley ever sexually abused that you know of?"

Maggie straightened her back and crossed her leg over her knee. She pushed her gum against the roof of her mouth. "No."

"I understand these are sensitive questions, Ms. Remick. Harley wasn't a lot of help with these things." Williams paused and wet his lips for his next question. "Did Harley ever take pleasure in killing animals or house pets that you're aware of?"

Maggie blinked quickly and tightened her jaw. "Not that I'm aware of, no. Do you think Harley is a serial killer or something? Is that who you're going to send me home with?"

"God, no, Ms. Remick. I don't think Harley is motivated to hurt anyone physically. It's just that patients tend to be evasive about answering questions like these honestly. Actually, they're not really standard questions."

"Then why are you asking them? Are you going to ask me how many times a day he masturbated?"

"No, of course not." Williams paused again. "Ms. Remick, is there a reason you didn't come to visit your son?"

"Harley lit my boyfriend's motorcycle on fire. He could have killed someone. My boyfriend left. I was upset, and there wasn't a lot I could do while I was paying the bills myself."

"I see. Does Harley's father have any type of role in his life?"

"Harley's father is a topic I don't want to think about. I

surely don't want to talk about it."

"I apologize Ms. Remick." Williams pulled a business card from the stack on the edge of his desk and wrote on the back. He handed it to Maggie. His fingers were long and thin, but thicker at a few of the knuckles as if he'd broken them before and they'd never healed properly. "My personal number is on the back if you ever want to talk about Harley or if there's anything you need to talk about." It took Maggie a moment to take his card because she was thinking of Harley, and how her break from him was over.

"Thank you."

"Are you okay, Ms. Remick? You look really pale."

"I'm fine. I think I just need some air."

"Okay. If you'd like, you can take Harley's things outside with you while you wait. He's already processing out. It shouldn't take too much longer. Ms. Remick, are you sure you're okay?"

"I'm fine."

Maggie scooped up Harley's box on her way out. She was glad to have something to carry in front of her when she walked past the guard. Outside, she put Harley's box on the passenger seat and lit a cigarette as she climbed in. Her hands trembled as she pulled the cigarette from her lips. In the rearview mirror, a hair-thin line of blue eyeliner worked its way down her cheek. She blew smoke at the mirror and turned it away.

SEVEN

When Harley emerged from the doors, a horrid cacophony of cursing and pounding came from the windows above him. It drew Maggie's attention to Harley, whose appearance shocked her. He'd grown half a foot. Nick's thin T-shirt wrapped tightly around Harley's chest and arms which had developed profile, firmness, muscle. The sharpened edge of his cheekbones cut through the memory she had of his round face. He kicked carelessly toward the car as he had when he was a child coming through the rush of children in grade school. Maggie stubbed out her cigarette in the ashtray and fumbled for the mirror. She smeared the running eye makeup from her face and swiped her hair from her forehead. Harley turned and waved at the boys in the windows making their cursing and pounding louder. She slipped her sunglasses back over her eyes and practiced a smile. Harley held up two middle fingers toward the boys then turned and climbed into the back seat.

"What are you doing?"

"Waving goodbye."

"No. What are you doing in the back seat?"

"I came here in a back seat. I'll leave in one."

His voice, too, was different. Deeper. Harder. Maggie wrapped her fingers around the shifter and pulled it down. Harley smelled different than she could remember. Like his voice, it hung around her like the crisp stroke of starched shirts against skin. He leaned over the seat and rummaged through his box. When he found the Zippo, he slumped into the back seat.

"You look different, Harley. I mean healthy. You look healthy." She blew a stream of smoke at the windshield.

Harley poked his finger into the plastic covering the window. He focused on his finger. "Yeah, Maggie. You look healthy, too."

"Are you happy to be going home?"

Harley sparked the flint on the Zippo. "Oh, yes. Home is a place that I've dreamed of the whole time I've been away." He closed the lighter. "You still with Nick?"

A twinge of nervousness quickened her heartbeat as she thought of Sean. "No, Harley. I haven't seen Nick since you went away. Were you hoping to see him?"

"I was hoping that maybe you'd have reunited with whoever my father is, and we could all be one big hap—"

"How about we change the fucking subject, hunh, Harley? Jesus Christ it hasn't been two minutes and you're already being a jerk."

Her hand shook as she reached for her pack of smokes on the dashboard. Empty. Harley leaned forward again and pulled his box into the back seat. A few miles down the road, Maggie pulled into a convenience store and hurried out of the car.

Inside the store, Maggie asked the clerk for two packs of light cigarettes. The clerk, his cheeks acne scarred, sucked his lips against his teeth as he navigated through the rows of cigarettes with his index finger. Maggie looked past him, through the neon *OPEN* sign out to her car. The man in the back seat of her car hardly resembled the son she'd had before he went to that place. Maybe it was good, she thought, that she hadn't visited.

Harley watched Maggie dig through her purse as she walked to the entrance. He was nineteen, had spent the downslope of his adolescence listening to the toughest kids he'd met crying, wetting themselves, begging for their mommies. He wrapped his stare around Maggie's legs and waist like the soft, cool denim she was wearing. She was smaller than he remembered—the neck, shoulders. Even the thickness of her legs seemed to have grown smaller, things he could wrap his hands around. Everything tapered to some point of convenient grip, contoured and structured as if physiologically designed for restraint. The bones were less dense than a man's and grew significantly more brittle with age. The profound genius of their bodies' mechanics, the ability to grow and nurture life from within their own body, only to be sprung from the womb to grow into the Aphroditic creature society molded them to be without the essential biological design for protection—a cruel flaw and proof that predatory instinct was based solely on the basis of evolutionary malfunction. Harley pushed himself back in his seat and felt a warm pressure coiling up his spine.

Maggie returned with her cigarettes, lighting one before she sank into the front seat and pulled the car back onto the road. Harley pulled his old clothes from the box, balled them up, and crammed them between his head and the door. He stretched his legs over the seat. It had been a long time since he'd slept in the back seat of a car, and he missed Maggie's. The shocks were gone on the driver's side and he liked how his feet would bounce from the seat when the car hit a pothole or speed bump too fast. He needed sleep and it came to him easily.

The door shut and woke him. Maggie bounded up the stairs to the apartment, her legs stretching as she took the four steps of the porch in two. Harley emerged from the car. Across the driveway, in the neighbor's front yard, a small boy began to cry. Another small boy, a bit bigger than the other, had just struck the boy's forehead with a stick. The crying was intolerable, and Harley stared at the child with an obvious look of disgust. A man came from the first-floor apartment and walked briskly to the boys. Bad posture, shirtless, beer gut, rebel flag tattoo, a dip in his lip, short hair, knotted knuckles and grease-stained fingers, green swim trunks. The man was a poster boy for Union Avenue.

"Daddy, he hit me," the small boy said, pointing at his brother.

"Get your ass in the fucking house," the father yelled, his voice deep and worn like a pair of old ten-dollar sneakers.

"But Dad, I didn't mean to," the other boy pleaded.

"Get in the goddamn house or I'll bash your fucking face in."

Harley laughed, loud, and the father turned toward him.

"What the fuck are you laughing at?" he asked Harley.

"You, tough guy."

The small boy had stopped crying and joined his brother in an awkward, open-mouthed stare at Harley.

"You talking to me, you piece of shit?"

"I'm not talking to the four-year-old."

"I'm five and a half," the boy said.

The father looked down at the boys then back to Harley. "Maybe you should mind your own business." Through his teeth he told them to get in the house. The boys obeyed and the father followed them, taking a few brooding glances at Harley.

Harley pulled the box from the car and slid his feet along the gravel in the driveway half hoping to see melted blots of leather. A few rocks in the driveway revealed slivers of the fire's memory. Harley felt his stomach muscles tighten, remembered the gut wrenching chill of the water that Nick had poured on him, how those furious seconds waiting to catch his breath made him feel as though rage and vengeance were waiting for his embrace. He remembered the sudden impact of the block of ice against his face, the plastic snapping sound between his ears. And he remembered all the times before that. His ribs and cheekbones returned the memory of their ache. Heat seemed to rise up as he stood remembering, like it had before, to dull the pain in his pounded flesh and bones.

He'd lived in that apartment most of his life among the different lovers his mother kept, lurking in corners and beneath the sheets of his bed wishing his mother would someday love him as much as she loved those other men—men who were wrong for her. None of her men ever had the ambition to love Harley as a son and he knew nothing of his father except that he looked like him—like a man his mother despised, which was the case for all of her men after they had taken what they'd wanted from her and moved on, leaving their odors and oil stains on the wood of the porch from their broken motorcycles.

Maggie came from inside tying the straps of her green apron behind her back. Her white collared shirt, a bit wrinkled in the back and along the sleeves, covered her cleavage. She backed out of the driveway. Harley ditched his box on the kitchen table when he went inside, ignoring the suede jacket over the back of a chair that belonged to his mother's new lover. He went to his room and pulled the snow globe from the windowsill. He'd missed it and the streetlight that reflected off the globe against the walls of his room at night. Shaking it, he followed the flecks twisting inside the glass.

Their talking woke him just after he'd fallen asleep. The male voice was quiet, an elevated pitch much different than what Harley expected and similar to Maggie's. Maggie giggled and Harley strained his eyes trying to hurry their adjustment to the darkness. They moved into Maggie's bedroom and he could no longer make out their words. The vibrations of their movement shook through the cracks and spaces of the floorboards and crept beneath his door. The noises and words blended together, like so many before that, and Harley lay still and quiet waiting for the weight of their bodies to shift from the floor onto the bed. Those first few moments after the shift Harley held his breath. He rolled his face into his pillow and exhaled, feeling the heat and moisture come back against his cheeks and over his ears.

EIGHT

The next morning, Harley peered from the doorway at the boy eating cereal at the kitchen table. His arms reminded Harley of the yardsticks the teachers had in grade school. They were made of foam, a precaution against rowdy boys sword fighting with them. The harder you swung them, the more they would bend, and it was impossible to injure anyone with them. A few strands of facial hair were scattered over the boy's face like thin, random marks of a pencil on a sheet of paper. His shoulders were dainty, almost elegant, and the thin fingers of his left hand held the spoon like a fragile piece of glass. Maggie stood at the sink sipping her coffee and froze for a moment, released a quick look of embarrassment, and looped her eyes away from Harley's stare.

"Who the fuck is this?" Harley asked.

The boy glared and hurried to swallow.

Maggie put her hand on Sean's shoulder and stood behind him. "This is Sean."

"Why is he eating your cereal?" Harley asked as he moved into the kitchen.

"Because I paid for it." Sean shoveled another spoonful into his mouth.

"Really? Did you buy the milk, too?"

Maggie studied the pit of her coffee cup.

"Are you running a daycare now?"

"I'm eighteen," Sean said.

Harley dramatized his look of surprise. "I guess that means you don't need a fucking permission slip."

Sean stood and went to the sink, his back on Harley. He lifted his bowl to his lips to finish the leftover milk and went into Maggie's room. *Their* room. The room that she had trial-run lovers in his whole life. It was the same with all the things in that apartment. The walls and doors and furniture remained the same. The only thing that changed was who walked through the doors and who sat on the furniture. Harley had aged, but all that surrounded him fell exactly where he remembered it every day he'd sat there staring at a new lover across the table since before his feet could touch the floor. Sean came from their room, one strap of his backpack draped over his shoulder. He kissed Maggie and slipped through the door. Maggie turned and moved Sean's bowl from the counter and placed it in the sink.

She spoke over her shoulder at him. Harley noticed two hickeys on either side of her neck that hadn't been there when she'd picked him up. "Does it bother you he's young?"

"Why should it bother me that my mother is sleeping with a guy younger than her son?"

Maggie turned and crossed her arms and looked through her bedroom door. "There's something else, something that you should know."

"What?"

She pulled the robe tighter around her breasts, where Harley was gazing. His eyes did not stray even when she leaned back and told him she was pregnant.

"Do you know who the father is?" Harley looked up at her face.

"Yes."

"That's a first."

"Fuck you, Harley."

Harley pointed toward the door. "He's not the father, is he?"

45

Maggie bit her lip and gripped the back of a chair.

"Seriously? What the fuck, Maggie?"

"What? Do you think just because he's young he can't be what I need?"

"Need? Does your little friend know his life's about to be over?"

"I can't tell him, yet. He's not ready for that."

"You mean he'll stop coming here after school to play house. He'll leave you and *your* baby. But I guess you're used to that."

Maggie dropped her mug into the sink and walked away from the clatter to the bathroom. Harley caught a glimpse of her breast down to the areola, and a bigger glimpse of the top of her thigh when the robe parted. He hated that there was nowhere else to go. There was no place to escape the torment of his mother's choices. He kept crawling back into the same still photo waiting for color or hope or love to change it somehow. *Why would she do this?* Sean would be difficult enough to accept, now that Harley was home again, but how would he accept a sibling whose father was younger than him? He went to the bathroom door and knocked.

"What do you want?" she asked.

He cleared his throat. "Have you thought about your options?"

"Options for what?"

He pressed his hairline against the door. His voice dropped. "Not having the baby."

The door flew open and his head nodded forward. "I should slap your face." She looked at him the way she had most of his life when he challenged what she wanted or couldn't have— hatred and blame, a self-enveloping pity that always seemed to bring something to her lips, but she never said it.

"You should get an abortion."

"Oh, that's nice."

"Exactly. A nice abortion."

Maggie shook her head and stared at his mouth.

"I'm not getting rid of this baby. It deserves a chance at life."

"That's why you should abort it."

She drew her head back. "Now why don't you think about that for a second, Harley. You're here."

"That's exactly my fucking point."

"No, Harley, what you're failing to see here is that it's time you made your own way. You're an adult now and living here isn't something that's going to work out. You need to find another place to live."

Maggie slammed the door and attempted to push her welling tears aside by pressing on her cheekbones. She sat on the edge of the tub squeezing the robe tightly around her. It took Harley a few minutes to move away from the door. He made a few trips across the length of the apartment before he left, and Maggie let her tears drop to the linoleum between her feet.

NINE

February 13, 1978

Maggie felt the weight against her spine—a pressure she yearned to spill out of her. Her ribs were sore and tired from heavy breathing, and despite the doctor's coaching, she couldn't focus on her breathing any longer, only the pain inside her working its way out. Her flesh like wet paper, but how it tore was nothing like paper. It ripped deep into her until it felt like her wounds had found their way to the bone. People had always told her that childbirth was a beautiful thing. She didn't think so. Everything about it felt ugly and cruel.

Dr. Walsh's fingertips brushed against the back of her hand—the doctor who had inspected her and verified her pregnancy months before. The others in the room, nameless, with no other connection to her than their responsibility to the task at that time, were nothing more than drones. Their voices muffled behind the masks they wore—a stoic light blue calm that draped over the bridge of their nose and covered their mouths. They'd pulled hundreds of babies from the womb, and Maggie blamed their presence for her pain.

"Get out," she cried. "Stop touching me and get out."

Some of them smiled at her outburst—their rising cheekbones projecting ridicule on Maggie. They smiled as the child tore from her, out of her, the way its father had torn his way in. She looked

48

through the room again hoping her mother would find just a few moments of mercy and be there for her. But Maggie could only see Edith the way that she'd looked at her during the past several months—a perpetual look of scorn splashed across Edith's face as if the sin had been committed against her.

Dr. Walsh's eyes were fixed but soft as the pain sent Maggie's focus in sharp sweeps over the room. The agony rushed through her in pulses. In her search for something to focus on, to shadow her mind's persistent grip on torment, she abandoned her hope in all that had been taught to her: that God loved her. That all suffering was a test of one's faith. Maggie found the dead eyes of a stuffed animal across the room.

The dying faded from the world on the floor below her. They exhaled the last sad sighs of their life as death tricked them with a blinding light that faded with their smiles and hopes of an afterlife. But there is no light beyond, and Maggie felt as if she could hear them cursing the life that had come out of her— violent, hateful cursing at the crying which became present in the room.

Stop its crying.

Stop its fucking crying.

Stop the crying. Take it away.

Shut that baby's fucking mouth.

As the pulse of Maggie's pain drifted away and the faces looking at her bore a different, silent expression, she realized the cursing was her own. Tears dropped away as she squeezed her eyelids, tears she could not label with an emotion. She let her legs go slack and they fell against the dampness of the mattress she lay on. The baby, held firmly by strong hands sheathed in latex, trembled with the chime of instruments used to cut the cord. A nurse took the baby and sponged it clean, then offered it to Maggie who turned her head away and curled her hands into fists against her chest.

Dr. Walsh cleaned his hands and made his way to the lobby where Maggie's mother sat. She stiffened her posture as he approached. He took a seat next to her, smiling at the child twisting in the chair across from him.

To his surprise, the woman spoke first. "She make it through?"

"She'll be fine. She's resting now."

"Well, I guess I should be going then."

"Mrs. Remick, Maggie's been through quite a bit. I'm sure she could use a loved one right now."

"She should have thought of that before she put herself into a situation to suffer the way she has."

Dr. Walsh sighed and cracked his knuckles against the insides of his knees. "I think the focus right now should be on the well-being of the child. You and Maggie might consider offering the child up for adoption."

"I'll hear nothing of the sort. I'm a single mother. I take care of my responsibilities. Margaret can do the same."

"Maggie's not ready to be a mother, especially under these circumstances."

"The problem with the world is that people shirk their responsibilities. They ignore the consequences of their actions and expect the rest of us to take care of them."

"I think the problem with the world is that there is a significant lack of compassion, Mrs. Remick." Dr. Walsh sighed as he stood. "Whose responsibility was it to keep something like this from happening to Maggie?"

TEN

Late Spring 1997

People gathered in small groups on the courthouse steps. A group of women, all of them bearing some blurred indigo forearm tat-too, smoked between chugs of Diet Pepsi. Men in sleeveless shirts stood at the edge of the sidewalk sizing Harley up as if he'd arrived to challenge them in some way. Harley widened his eyes as they stared at him, catching glimpses of their teeth as the men worked their lips over blackened rot, squinting at him and widening their shoulders. Harley thought of steel wool and nine-volt batteries, the smell that erupted into the air just before the nine-volt ignited the steel wool. He could almost see it at the back of their throats, where that smell was coming from behind puffs of cigarette smoke.

Down the street, a more organized handful of people circled a building. The sun bore into his eyes as he tried to read their signs. Picketers, and Harley remembered that there was a women's clinic close to the courthouse. And he only knew that because of the taunts in junior high when the other kids told him that his mother should have stopped there instead of the hospital. Sweat soaked his chest before he turned from the chants of the picketers and made his way into the courthouse.

The smell of the lobby rushed toward him—diluted cleaners, secondhand clothes, wet wood, and hot rubber. The first day of school always smelled like brand new T-shirts, not that he'd ever pulled open a package of Hanes or Fruit of the Loom, but he'd always smelled it on the other kids. Unlike those first days of school, the courthouse always smelled like a mix of lost and found or Salvation Army.

Harley pulled the papers from his pocket, the business card for his probation officer. The black ink was simple aside from the gloss. The lower right corner was bent and the card was crinkled down the center. The papers were damp with sweat from his walk there. *Darnell Milkner, Probation Officer.* Harley looked up at the directory, the white, plastic letters and the spacing and straightness of them. Milkner's office was in the basement.

The courthouse had been recently renovated except for the basement. The basement corridor was a dim cavern. Traffic, janitorial neglect, and the trailing remnants of the town's dregs left their filth and stench in the hall. Cigarettes, mildew, sweat, wet shoes all lingered somewhere on the dull tile walls and floor. He found Darnell Milkner's office and stood breathing close to the man's nameplate on the right side of the door.

Milkner's face was pockmarked and red. His nose was puffy and his teeth were stained and vicious, like he crawled into the ground at night and soaked them in mud. The office was floored with dark carpet and Harley hated the look of the chair Milkner wanted him to sit in. Beat and haggard as if it'd been dragged behind Darnell's vehicle from his house to his office. The chair's legs had rubbed through the shitty carpet and dug into the cement. The corners of the desk were missing the plastic veneer that covered the particle board. White scuff marks slashed across the black metal front of the desk from the cheap shoes people had worn in that office. Harley'd burned furniture that was left in better shape. The office had been freshly painted a soft yellow. Harley could smell it, welcomed it over the odor. A box holding the contents of whatever Milkner had kept on the walls rested in the corner behind him.

Milkner grumbled while he exerted effort to pull Harley's file from a lower drawer in the filing cabinet beside his desk. "Have a seat," he prompted again. The man grunted and Harley cringed as he sat. "Been reading up on you. Bet you like marshmallows, eh kid?"

Harley tilted his head. "No."

"Well, that's probably good. Maybe it'll keep you from starting any more blazes." Each movement the man made, regardless of how subtle, resulted in a grunt, and Harley began to count them. Harley became obsessed with counting and it reminded him of his first fire—counting the seconds that a sheet of paper burned, twenty-three. He was so overwhelmed with the numbers that Milkner's grumbling voice faded to the sound of a crackling blaze, like a wheezing inhale, the soft transformation of paper to ash and its whispering collapse.

"Do you understand why you're here?"

Harley nodded.

Milkner peered over his glasses, the metal frames cutting painful lines through his sideburns. "Yes, eh, well, they said you were a quiet one."

Harley smirked.

"Well, enough with the formalities. You're here because you got in trouble. You've paid the consequences with your placement in a youth facility, but we're still going to keep some tabs on you. Tell you what, though. You're lucky you went OCFS. I see a lot of boys even younger than you were who went straight to jail. You're lucky no one was hurt. But that was the past and you're here to focus on your future. Now, the state requires you to find a job, take monthly urine tests, and make your appointments on time. Are you going to have any trouble with that?"

Harley shook his head.

"Well, you might if you don't learn better communication skills. Have you lined up a job?"

"No."

"That's generally the case. I've got something for you, but it's no nine to five. You'll have early morning hours and you'll be around teenagers. That a problem for you?"

Harley hesitated, trying to remember the number. "Nineteen."

"Hunh? No, not likely. These are high school kids. Fourteen to eighteen, usually."

"Twenty-one."

"Twenty-one-year-old high schooler might need to reevaluate his position in academics."

"High school? How is it possible that I'm going to be able to work at a high school with, well, with my previous experience in the system?"

"It's a custodial position. And your record will remain a sealed juvenile record, provided you keep your nose clean for the next two years. You don't have to disclose any criminal charges that you were found guilty of as a minor. The hours are six a.m. to three p.m. You get an hour lunch." Milkner tore a sheet of paper from his notepad and handed it to Harley. "Ms. Oumba will be expecting you on Friday for your interview. Don't be late. I'll see you on the," Milkner cleared some papers to look at his desk calendar, "twenty-fifth."

"Twenty-seven."

"No. The twenty-seventh is Friday. I don't meet probation on Fridays. The twenty-fifth. Nine in the morning." Milkner handed Harley a pen. "You might want to write that down. Nine o'clock."

Harley took the pen from the man's short, stubby fingers. They were hairy and Harley awed at them, how they looked trollish. Harley wrote the date and time and slipped the pen back on Milkner's desk to avoid touching his hand.

Harley took a deep breath when he got outside. Clouds scurried past the sun. He turned his palms up toward its heat and stared at the glistening sheen of sweat in the lines on his palms. The bus pulled to a halt at the end of the street, a hundred feet from the courthouse. A few people emerged carrying signs and made their way toward Harley. He turned his head to read their signs as they passed—biblical citations and *murder* written in red marker were the most that he could make out as they hurried past him.

ELEVEN

Picketers gaggled and bobbed their signs up and down: *Abortion is murder! Life is precious! Thou shalt not kill! Killing is wrong.* Harley wondered if any of them had heard of the Midianites. He noticed the women in the crowd, women who might have had a different perspective if they had been raped or molested or had fallen victim to some other kind of dominance that men inflict on women. Most of them looked like college students. The picketers presented an idea that women sought the termination to make their life easier, that they weren't thinking about the kid. Sometimes the kid was better off never being a kid at all. Some of them held bibles, the book that told stories of men sacrificing their children for God, slitting a human's throat to please the will of an infallible Holy Ghost. Not to mention that unlucky motherfucker who was so precious only a virgin could bear him, whom God let dangle from the cross after torture and unimaginable agony. Their eyes berated Harley like pelted stones as he made his way past them to the walkway of the clinic.

He felt the swath of chaotic heat around him similar to when he left the boys' home—hot breaths of anger from all directions. But where did the anger come from? Why were they angry? Harley wondered. It was easy for him to acknowledge the anger in the boys he left behind. It was obvious jealousy. But here, why? What did those people have to be angry about? That they didn't abort a child who possibly hated them? That they couldn't have a child? Were those precious lives meant to be spared so those people could go through the formalities of adoption? To be that child's savior? *They* were the answer? Were there not enough children already who could be loved, who those people could share time with instead of butting heads with the inevitable? Harley's inner questioning, which he could not manage to ration, was interrupted by a middle-aged woman whose sneer burned through the jabbing of his thoughts. Plaque rode at the edges between her teeth, and she wore a formless green dress that dragged against the pavement behind her heels.

"You're making her do it, aren't you? You're making her a murderer. It's always a man who pushes this on women."

"Of course it's a man. How else would she get pregnant?"

"You're wrong for making her do it," she said.

Harley took a moment to study her, the vacant look in her eyes, her assumptions. "It's better than pushing her down the stairs. That hardly ever kills anyone, and there's a good chance that she'd live, and I'd end up in prison. A third-story window would be ideal, or even a fire escape or a rooftop. There are trains, tractor-trailers, and buses that I could have shoved her in front of, and boy, did I think about all those opportunities on the way here. There are other ways, of course, to make it look like an accident, but those are far more complicated."

"You're a goddamn monster..."

"Thank you. Have a wonderful day."

Harley moved past the woman and into the clinic, where a secretary bulged in turquoise scrubs behind the front desk. Two nurses stood on either side of her, pointing at a piece of paper. The place smelled like vinyl gloves and bandages.

"Excuse me," he said to the woman.

The secretary turned to him. "Are you here for a patient?"

"Not exactly."

The phone rang, and she answered it, holding up her index finger to him, and the nurses moved on to other tasks. Harley turned to the waiting room full of mismatched chairs and end tables, and a nearly empty jug of water resting crooked in the water cooler. Another space that was identical except for the people sitting in the chairs, a room with little light and no toys full of people trying to make up for the mistakes they made. Three people sat in different corners of the waiting room. One girl sucked in a shuddering breath between sobs. Harley couldn't help but feel that she was doing a horrible job at keeping her emotions to herself—crying once for a child she would probably only provide a life of misery for. Another girl was tense and staring at the sobbing girl across the room. The one man in there sat by the wall between the two girls and kept most of his attention on the ceiling. Harley slid into the seat beside the crying girl.

"First time?" he asked.

She stopped crying and shook her head. Her face tightened and her lips moved to speak. As the first syllable of the word she'd found began to come out of her mouth, Harley cut her off.

"Ah, quiet. Finally. Let's keep it up."

Harley moved across the room away from a slower sobbing.

"Come here often?" he asked.

The man dropped his stare at the ceiling, blinked, and gawked at Harley.

"Are you fucking serious?" the girl asked.

"Harley. I'm Harley. Place would be a lot more conducive to conversation with some of those HELLO, MY NAME IS stickers on our chests."

"You're an absolute lunatic. Of course." She leaned away from him and crossed her legs. A few nubs of hair stuck to the shaving nick just behind her ankle.

"Are you having a rough one? Maybe I could take you for an ice cream cone when you're done here."

"Seriously, get the fuck away from me."

The secretary hung up her phone.

"Sir, I can help you now."

Harley sauntered to the front desk.

"How can I help you?"

"My mother's pregnant and I want her to have an abortion."

She expressed a look of curiosity and shook her head. "Um. You'll have to discuss that with your mother. Is this a joke?"

"No joke, butterball."

Her head flinched and she batted her eyes.

"She's pregnant and the father is younger than I am."

"Your mother will have to come in here herself."

"Obviously. It's not like I can bring her the abortion. How much is this going cost?"

"It depends."

"Does insurance cover it?"

"No. Now, unless you have any more legitimate questions, I'm going to have to ask you to leave."

"Okay, but since I'm already here, would it be possible to purchase a gift certificate?"

The secretary lowered her chin and peered at Harley through her furrowed brow. "For an abortion?"

"Yeah...Haven't you been listening to anything I've said?"

"Okay." The secretary picked up her phone. "I'm calling the police now unless you leave this building."

Harley crept around the picketers on his way out, glancing up at their signs once more. He passed the grocery story that Maggie worked at on his way back to her place. The sting of her words was beginning to wear off, but he was still choking down the rage that had set his perspective ablaze. Signs in the window offered buy-one-get-one-free deals. A glow of cleverness spread through his mind and he marched home.

Maggie was occupying herself in the living room with soap operas. She lay on the floor on her stomach, leaning into her palms and made no attempt to acknowledge Harley as he passed. Harley noticed then how often their interaction had been closer to sibling disdain. It was even more evident now that he'd had some time away from Maggie.

Harley found a black marker and went into his room. He dumped the contents of the box he'd carried from the boys' home and ripped the flaps from the sides. The slogans he wanted to write on his poster board to protest with the other picketers at the clinic worked themselves out in his mind. He placed the snow globe on the cardboard to gauge the size of his letters and dusted the torn, cardboard particles from the panel. Carefully, he etched out the letters of his slogan with pencil, traced over them with the black marker, and colored in the letters. The markers began to smell like gasoline and made him dizzy.

"Harley." His mother opened his door. Harley looked over at the waistband of her jeans where it rode low on her hips and the curve of her abdomen sloped downward above the bone to the top button that was undone. "I have to open tomorrow. I'll need you to make sure Sean is up for school."

"Why do I have to be his alarm clock?"

"You're nineteen, Harley. I'll let you stay here until you find a job, but when you are here, you're going to have to pull some weight."

"How much weight does he pull, aside from you on top of him?"

"Don't be an asshole. He needs to be up by seven thirty."

"I'm not being an asshole. The kid is going to be a father and he can't even get himself up in the morning?"

"Harley, I mean it. And don't say a word about that. I want the time to be right when I tell him."

"Your kid will be a freshman when that time comes."

Maggie shook her head and walked away, leaving the door open.

"Should I pack his lunch too?"

Maggie left the house to pick up Sean from school. His early release allowed them time to cruise around town and smoke cigarettes. It made her feel younger, like she was sharing an experience with Sean that she'd missed out on, the beginning stages of options, choosing things that she wanted to do instead of shuffling back into the life she had with Harley. She took the long, twisting road down to parking lot at the back of the high school where the teachers and staff parked, where Sean insisted that she pick him up. She spotted him as she passed the student parking section. He was strutting, his backpack draped over his shoulder and another, which Maggie guessed belonged to the girl he was walking with, he held at his side bouncing it casually off his knee.

The girl shook her head to waft her hair from her face as she slipped on a pair of sunglasses. The hem of her khaki shorts tightened around her muscular thighs as she walked. Thick, pale legs flexed with a brutish demeanor. Her arms, too, were thick, but lacked the muscle tone of her legs. Her face was round and unattractive and her ears were mousy, standing out from the side of her head. While Maggie listed the girl's imperfections, the girl stumbled over a small rock and lost her balance. Sean caught her in an embrace, his thin arms wrapped low around her waist. He'd dropped her backpack and one of the flip-flops the girl was wearing rested upside down on the pavement.

For the moment that the two teenagers were in each other's arms, Maggie held a breath of cigarette smoke. It slipped through the corner her slightly opened mouth. What could have been nothing but a simple reaction, a reflex to reach out and keep someone from falling, was utterly perturbing Maggie until the cigarette had burned down to her finger. She cursed aloud, snatching the attention of a departing faculty member, and shook her hand out the window to discard the cigarette. A pair of eyes set gently in the skull of a gray bearded man peered over horn-rimmed glasses at her. She immediately inserted the burned knuckle of her left index finger into her mouth and simultaneously turned her hand up and palm out in an effort to hide her face. Sean kept an arm around the girl and helped her to her car.

Sean handed the girl the backpack through the open window and strutted across the lawn. Maggie's hand quivered when she released the steering wheel to reach over and unlock the passenger door. She noticed his gait, the false confidence much like the way he'd strolled up to ask for a cigarette when they'd first met. When Sean climbed into the car, Maggie already had it in gear and began to pull out of the parking spot before he'd shut the door.

"You in a hurry?" he asked her.

Maggie rolled through the stop sign and sped up toward the back entrance of the high school. Students moved down the sides of the road toward their cars or in small groups to whatever after school destination they had decided on during lunch or one of their classes. Some of them had lit cigarettes and held them discreetly at their sides.

"Are you going to answer me?"

Maggie stopped the car to make a right turn onto the main road. She shook a cigarette from her pack and let the pack fall to the floorboard. Sean reached down and flung it on the dash.

"What is your problem, Maggie?"

"Nothing, Sean," Maggie mumbled over her cigarette puffing large clouds of smoke. "Absolutely nothing."

"That's bullshit. If nothing is wrong, then why are you driving fifty in a thirty-five?"

Maggie glanced down at the speedometer and tapped the brakes to slow the vehicle. Her cigarette burned down the bottom half, leaving the top to look like a mangled board left after a structure fire. Sean scratched the inside of his leg.

"Maggie?"

"What, Sean?" She glared at him then brought her focus back to the road and flattened her hair over the ridge of her forehead.

"You're obviously pissed at something. What the fuck is it?"

"You really want to know. I sit boiling in this car waiting for you and you take your sweet ass time getting over to me.

Sometimes I feel like your taxi and your fuck doll."

"Well, you are quite the doll. And it's not quite that hot out."

"Yeah? And you're not quite a fuck, either."

"You would know, wouldn't you?"

"I'm sure that bitch you were hugging on would too."

"Jesus, is that what this is about? It's not even like that."

"Then what was it then?"

"We're in class together. I asked if I could copy her notes."

"Yeah? And were you carrying her backpack as some sort of favor return?"

"Basically. It's no big deal. Calm down."

"I'm calm, Sean. Believe me, I'm calm."

Maggie careened into the driveway, unleashing her seat belt before the car stopped. She turned the car off and fumbled with her bracelet caught on the shifter. When she freed herself, she drove the shifter into park, spun from the car, and slammed the door. Maggie tossed her purse onto the table where Harley sat with his chin resting on his folded hands, watching a fly twitch on the mouth of an empty soda bottle. The fly buzzed from the bottle in a spiral in front of her face, and she swatted at it with both hands until she found the quiet of her bedroom and kicked the door closed.

TWELVE

When Sean sauntered through the kitchen to follow Maggie, Harley slid quietly from the chair and walked to his room. The two walls that separated Harley's room from the bathroom and then Maggie's room were too thin and inadequate to completely muffle the sounds of their argument. That was Maggie's pattern. There'd be an argument, which would subside with a brief quiet until a different type of madness would seep through the house. Maggie would leave the room and shower while her lover bobbed into the kitchen with a gluttonous pride quickly satisfied by whatever food or beverage he found in the refrigerator. The same sounds were always there, the meat-slapping sound of fucking or eating.

The sounds of the night wrapped tightly around him like the winter coats he had to wear as a child even after he'd outgrown them. Crickets—he tried to count them by their individual chirping, and at first he was doing well to keep track of their location in the yard. As the streetlights seemed to strike harder at the night, the chirping grew more until it was a subdued, vibrating shriek that drove Harley to fury. He closed the window and folded his arms over the sides of head when he buried his face into the thin pillow.

In the morning, Harley woke early to work on cardboard signs for the abortion clinic protest. Maggie showered and got herself ready for work—medicine cabinet closing, plastic covers falling into the sink, the sound of her saying *shit*. Pounding on the floor that he recognized as her hopping on one foot as she pushed her legs through her pants. Jars rattled in the refrigerator door, then it shut. Keys jingled as she moved through the door. When she pulled out of the driveway, Harley slipped into her room. Sean dug around in the front of his boxers and his penis slid through the front slit. His hair was disheveled, and Harley thought of the teenage pranks he could pull—shaving cream in the hand and tickling his nose or putting Sean's hand in a bowl of cold water. Or was it warm water? He tried to remember.

Harley wrote Sean an excuse for being late: *Please excuse Sean from being late. He was being molested.* He signed the letter illegibly and waited until he was sure Sean would be late for school before slamming his mother's door open and screaming inches from Sean's face: "Wake up. You're late for school." Sean scrambled away from Harley, leaving the putrid odor of his breath to linger in Harley's face. Harley waited at the table for Sean to explode from the room.

"Maggie wrote you a note in case you were late."

Sean snatched the sealed envelope from Harley as he charged through the door.

Harley slipped a pillowcase over his picket sign that he had taped to the bristles of the broom. He found an old cub scout baseball hat in his closet. He'd never been a cub scout. He tried to remember where it had come from. The hat barely fit, and Harley wished he'd had the whole outfit. He left the apartment, shaky with what he was about to do.

At the clinic, the picketers were flocked into their group. The scuffing of their shoes pattered amidst the chanting, and Harley imagined the hypocrisy they hid—the dark, shameful secrets they must have had. The Born Again hoisted her sign which read: *A Life is Precious* while her womb hid in her body mutilated from a series of terminations. One man carried a bible instead of a sign, using it as his excuse to judge women even though his homosexuality would never put him in danger of making that choice. Even the woman who had confronted Harley the day before had a secret of her own, the abandonment of her spouse and their child two decades before. A secret that would have balled up her truculent accusations against Harley the day before and cemented them in her throat had it been exposed. Guilt brought her to God, and religion allowed that guilt to transcend into judgment and stupidity with the assumption that she was forgiven.

Sunlight peeked over the dome of the courthouse where Harley had met with his probation officer. The pavement clutched heat while rays of fleeing light surged from the minerals embedded in the tar. Harley pulled the pillowcase from his sign. His palms sweat as he held it with a weak grip that made the polished blue lacquer of the handle slip in his hands. The picketers' chants hovered in the air around him until the sparks of Harley's memory brought him back to North Falls and the boys' indignant howls from inside the building. He dried his hands against his pantleg, alternating his grip on the sign, and made his way into the crowd. A soft breeze wimpled the edges of as the cardboard as he pushed it up and down into the air. The letters were darker—a square, bold font that read:

BUY ONE GET THE SECOND HALF OFF.

To Harley, their commitment to their cause was false glory. They changed nothing. They were jackals—panhandlers for humiliation. They pointed fingers and cupped whispers into ears. They were hollow. They didn't volunteer at youth organizations or battered women's shelters or support victims of rape or attempt any proactive action to help eliminate the reasons women got abortions. They were cold, cowardly fucking hypocrites with too many fingers to point, and too much breath. They were bored animals who no longer had to hunt and gather, but the instinct was still there. They hunted causes, something to satisfy the conscience, what evolution had given them. They picked sides, often simply to oppose another, to fight. They used volume to validate their opinions, their primal motives bullying out logic and compassion.

It took several minutes for anyone to notice Harley's sign. The woman who confronted Harley previously shuffled from the circle and stalked toward him. She slipped from the opposing picketer traffic. The lines in the skin above her thin lips formed delicate wrinkles against her pale skin—a soft curtain before the sacrificial pit. She slipped her hand around the handle of Harley's sign just before he was about to thrust it toward the sky.

"What are you trying to do?" she asked.

"Get your damn hands off my sign, lady," he said, pulling it from her grip.

The woman let her sign fall to the ground like a muffled insult. Again, she reached for Harley's sign, wrapping her fingers around the handle between his hands. "Bastard," she hissed and pulled the sign to her chest.

"Bitch," Harley rebutted and pulled his sign back.

The picketers, in losing their cadence, formed a circle around Harley and the woman. Their chant dissipated into the rising humidity. Their movement slowed as if they were trying to find their way in the fog, fear stripping their throats of the ability to call for their leader. The woman's forearms tensed. Her expression tighten as she processed her efforts. She pulled at the sign again, even harder than before, and Harley let the tension increase for a moment and let the sign go.

She smashed the handle of the sign against her face. Blood trickled in a thin line to her top lip. The signs around him lowered toward the ground. Without clearing the tangled hair from her vision, the woman lifted his sign, a prophet ready to smash stone tablets, and swung it toward Harley who slipped to the side, and the woman sprawled forward into the pavement. Harley tried to push through the picketers who had closed their distance on him and tripped over the chaos of shoes.

Harley scrambled from them against the ground, barely gaining his balance before he made it across the street. The picketers stood there for a minute, pointing down at Harley's slogan on the cardboard and the woman and then at him. One of the other picketers chucked the sign javelin style in his direction. The broom stick tore away from his sign when it hit the street. It was the only victory they could celebrate.

A few of the women had emerged from the clinic to observe the disruption, including a couple nurses. They stood together in a small front with one hand on their hip and another across their brows to shade the sun. The group reformed and continued with their chants. A girl hurried toward the clinic and the picketers pointed their fingers and shouted *murderer*. Harley wondered if Maggie would have had the courage to keep going. The girl covered her face and went inside the clinic where it was safe.

The picketers reassembled and unified their chant. Harley set his shoulders, straightened his back, and blew his breath out at the heat. Their efforts were empty, unfulfilling, like offering a hungry stomach prayer instead of food. Abortion gave them purpose. Whores gave them purpose, until Jenny got knocked up by the gardener, or Susie got gang-banged at a frat party, or Mom's extramarital affair would be an embarrassment to the family, or Senator Shithead impregnated a minor. Excuses were only valid if you were a hypocrite.

THIRTEEN

Two girls tossed ninety-nine-cent snacks on the conveyer at Maggie's register. Swiss rolls, Little Debbies, Zebra Cakes, and Star Crunches. They each placed a liter of diet cola behind their snacks. The girls wore nylon leggings with gym shorts over them. Sports bras under their tank tops, and their hair pulled tightly into ponytails. Typically, Maggie would let the girls pass through her line without giving notice, but Sean's interaction with his peer and the girls' mention of prom prompted Maggie's suspicion of Sean.

"Oh, it's that time of year again already?"

"What time of year?"

"For prom."

"Oh, totally. Did they even have prom when you were in school?"

Both girls giggled and brought their foreheads together.

Maggie finished sliding the girls' snacks over the scanner. She scooped them up in her hands, forced her thumbs into the softness of their texture and dropped them into a plastic bag.

"Ooh. Diet," Maggie said holding up the sodas. "Better be sure to fit in those dresses, girls."

"Excuse me?"

Maggie flicked a button and their total flashed in digital red letters on the register. She read the total aloud and snatched the ten-dollar bill from the girl's hand.

"Happy purging, ladies."

Maggie handed their change back, turned off her register, and pulled the key. She walked toward the break room before the girls had a chance to recover from her insult.

Maggie sat in the break room taking small bites off a Twizzler and scanned the pages of a women's exercise magazine. Women in dresses. Toned and slender legs. Breasts full and perky. Tan. At the mirror on the wall beside the lockers, Maggie unbuttoned her shirt and cupped her breasts. She pushed up on them, pressed them together and bit her lip as they settled lower when she pulled her hands away. Maggie buttoned her shirt and turned back to the table and her magazine.

The presence of him startled her. Her body shook with a violent shudder and her fingers latched onto the collar of her shirt. Mr. Tobias, the grocery store manager who had his own office on the other side of the store, and no reason to be there, stood beside the break room door.

"You scared the fucking shit out of me."

Tobias thumbed his shirt tighter into his belt line. "I'm sorry, there, Margo." He chuckled and laced his fingers together in front of his belt buckle.

She hated it when he called her "Margo." Maggie shook her head and took her seat back at the table. She filched a magazine from the stack and flipped through the pages with determination to keep herself from acknowledging him more.

Tobias was short and carried the grace of a dying, limp flower. He was soft, doughy, and seemed to fill his clothes much like batter in a cupcake wrapper. The only confidence he had was what his authority provided him at the store. He was cordial and lived alone with parakeets and fish, often bringing out mundane, anecdotal tales of how he once fed his parakeets fish food or how he'd broken the fishbowl one afternoon and let them swim in his bathroom sink for a week. He'd come on to Maggie before, trying to gain her excitement by detailing the board games he played or the game shows he liked to watch, then suggesting she join him some time. He tried hard to get his employees to like him, but the employees only took opportunities to mock his eccentric gestures and take advantage of his passive nature. He was nothing like his father, who'd hired Maggie, and died several years later only to leave the business in the hands of his son.

Tobias looked around the room. In that time, Maggie had gone through two magazines and started on her third—a prolonged, awkward agony.

Tobias's voice finally broke the sound of flipping pages. "So, Maggie, I was wondering if you'd be interested in some overtime."

"What days?"

"I need someone to cover Carolyn's shift on Sunday. That will put you on—"

Maggie cut him off. "Opening or closing?"

"Well, both, actually."

Maggie slapped the magazine on the table. "I'll let you know tomorrow. Break's over."

She went back out to her register. Tobias flapped his arms and puttered a breath through his lips as she passed.

Maggie spent the rest of her shift taking short bathroom breaks to adjust her bra in an attempt to pull her breasts higher. Tobias wandered through the store nodding to customers and giving them a pleasant hello when they acknowledged his gesture. He stole glimpses at Maggie from time to time, which Maggie noticed, and began to wonder about. He seemed to hover in her general area, adjusting bags of chips and fluffing the loaves of bread. She thought more about his request and wondered if he were testing her in some way.

Maggie hurried from work at the end of her shift but sat in her car long enough to smoke three cigarettes. Prom, she thought, and realized she knew nothing about the adolescent event except for the garbage she saw on poorly scripted comedies, and Stephen King's infamous *Carrie*. Pig's blood. She wanted to spray those two little cunts down with it. Sean hadn't mentioned prom, though. Even if he weren't going, she was sure he would have mentioned his disinterest. Maggie grew furious with thoughts of Sean and the girl he'd walked to her car. Quickly, though, her anger subsided and she was deluged with insecurity. She pinched at the skin on her hips, pulled at the inseam of her jeans to test their tightness. She studied the vague lines at the corners of her eyes and lips. Before she realized it, her thoughts so stitched to her focus she'd forgotten the drive home, she was pulling in her driveway.

Harley was at the kitchen table drawing flames over the heads of people in the local newspaper with a red Sharpie. Maggie stripped her shirt off in her room, and her bra. Her bedroom door hadn't latched when she closed it, and it crept open. She stood in front of the mirror cupping her breasts and biting the inside of her cheek. Maggie let her breasts fall to their natural position then lifted them again. When she dropped her hands to her sides and saw Harley in the mirror, staring over the newspaper through the thin opening, she threw her hand across her chest, turned, and shut her door.

Maggie sat on her bed pondering Harley's stare. She attempted to convince herself that he was spacing, that he wasn't focused on her nakedness. Had she seen what she thought she saw? Was his hand moving beneath the table? No. He wasn't spacing. The stare was too intense. Sean had bore that look for her once. The eyes, Harley's eyes had focused on her with such intensity that it made her question Sean, and his declining affection and interest in her body.

The kitchen door burst open and Sean's voice was loud.

"You think you're pretty goddamn funny, don't you?"

"What are you talking about?" Harley asked.

"That note, you fucking prick. I got three days in-school suspension."

Maggie pulled a T-shirt over her head and went into the kitchen. "What is going on out here?"

"This fucking prick," Sean said, pointing at Harley, "wrote

me a late excuse that said I was being molested."

"Jesus Christ, it was only a joke. Don't be so sensitive. Now go do your homework before bedtime."

"Harley, really? Do you have to be like that all the time?"

"What? What happened? What'd I do?"

Maggie pulled Sean into her room.

"I'm not fucking kidding, Maggie. He's going to get punched."

"If you think that's going to do anything, Sean, you're wrong. You need to calm down. He's not going to be here much longer."

"What do you mean, calm down? He embarrassed me."

"Sean, just forget that for a minute, please." Maggie stripped off the T-shirt she'd thrown on and studied Sean's reaction. "There's a better way to handle this." She moved closer to him and opened the button on his pants. "Let it go, baby," she whispered. His ear had the taste of salt and she felt him swell in her hand. "I need you to fuck me. Fuck me hard."

Harley went to his own room biting his lip until he could free his erection from his pants. It hurt, the throbbing. After a while, Maggie's bed springs began to whine. Harley imagined her naked and sprawled on the bed guiding him inside her and telling him how to move, to go slow. He felt a hammer-pounding throb between his eyes and through his groin. Sean's grunting in the next room made him squeeze the Zippo in his pocket. Flames. In his mind he saw them wrap around the sounds he could hear until he saw them, Maggie and Sean in the fuck-heap on their bed with flames climbing up the sheets. Harley pulled out his erection and wiped spit from his tongue to rub himself. He smelled smoke and felt the same heat from that first fire he started. Maggie whimpered in the next room and he came hard, staggering into the bedpost. The soft drops of his ejaculate hit the floor.

Harley went to sleep that night with the image of the embryo floating inside Maggie like the white flecks inside his snow globe. The life the child would have, he thought, of nothing to look forward to but the shame and misery of a life wondering why the person who was supposed to love him didn't and learning they never would. And Sean, he was nothing more than a vigil to the youth Maggie wanted to regain—the part of her life that he had spoiled. This was her second chance, her chance to do things right. What about his chance? He didn't even get one. Why should she have a second? It seemed selfish how she would create life in an attempt to redeem herself. He thought of the picketers and the women they may have intimidated into having children they didn't want and never would.

FOURTEEN

The morning air was cool, but the brightness of the light climbing the branches of the trees that Harley walked beneath would soon eliminate the sense of comfort he enjoyed. The time he'd spent away from his hometown seemed less lengthy as he passed buildings and empty lots he'd neglected to notice before the boys' home. The abandoned buildings were still abandoned, tattooed with red squares and a white X through them. Some of them had dilapidated more. Some were reduced to rubble. Some were simply gone, leaving sand and broken blocks of cement where they'd once stood, as if pinched from the earth during the night. Various pieces of litter, plastic bags and candy wrappers and soda bottles, stuck through the tight branches of hedges that he passed. Condom wrappers and broken glass and cigarette butts paled under the sun in the gutters. As he walked to his interview at the high school, Harley thought about how Limington, New York, made him feel like a piece of chewing gum stuck to the underside of a park bench. Over time, it becomes fused to the bench, a part of it—nothing but a smudge from something discarded because it lost its flavor. Like him, nothing but a stain on the underbelly.

He walked the slight decline in the side road that led to his former high school. The tar on the edges of the road had crumbled against the eroding dirt, a snake-like path along the side where rainwater had flowed. Nervousness. He'd have to answer questions about his work history and why he'd make a good employee, what qualifications and experience he had that would benefit the custodial department if they hired him.

The secretaries lingered in the main office. Three of them, all leaning in on various furniture and fixtures behind the counter—a desk, a filing cabinet, the side counter where late students requested passes for class. They wore turtlenecks and pink blouses and polyester blend pants, the plastic-looking shoes that nurses wore in the slasher films Harley enjoyed. They wore gold wedding bands and talked about their husbands' ailments—arthritis, knee surgery, hemorrhoids. Harley interrupted their conversation and sips of coffee to inform them of his interview. The woman closest to him had him sign in on the visitor sheet and spat out some directions, then returned to finish a description of her husband's crooked fingers. Harley signed the sheet: *Johnny Oar.*

The interview Milkner had set up for him placed him in a cold, ceramic school chair before a hefty, black woman with short hair and a light blue shirt with *Bruno* embroidered in white thread that had taken on the brownish-yellow stains and colors from her duties. Her skin was dark and dull like everything else about her except her hair. He couldn't get over her hair and how the light above them glinted in the strands.

"You can mop?" she asked him. Her voice was deep, and her words came out clumsy as they tripped over her understanding of the language. It reminded Harley, for some reason, of when he was a child and sucked the air inside a plastic cup to hold it against his face.

"If it's dirty, I can clean it." Harley thought of his days at the boys' home—buffing the floors and the smell of bleach haunting him into the night hours after the floors had dirtied again. He handed her his application.

Bruno looked it over, dragging a thick sweaty digit over the ink. She paused on his work experience where there wasn't anything written down.

"You never work?" she asked him.

"I've been in training for the last several years."

"Train for what?"

"The Olympics."

"Olympics?" Bruno pushed back in the chair and stroked her lips with her tongue.

"Yeah. The special kind."

Harley bit his bottom lip to keep himself from smiling.

"What you do? Run? Swim?"

"Curling. That's why my cleaning skills are so incredible."

"You no longer do this?"

Harley lifted his left hand gingerly and rubbed the wrist with his right hand. "No," he answered. "I fell asleep on my hand one night and strained the tendons in my wrist. The precision is gone."

Bruno furled her brow. "This is lie. Why you lie?"

Harley lowered his hands and looked back at her. "I don't have any work experience because I've been in placement for the last two years."

"Placement?"

"You know, juvy."

"I see."

"Miss Bruno. I was really only trying to make you laugh. I didn't mean to upset you. I really need this job."

"Later, you tell funny stories. Not lies. We go smoke. Then I show your stuff."

Bruno led him to the boiler room. As he passed through the hallways, he remembered the time he'd spent pushing through to get to classes he hated, staying close to the sickly green tile spaced between orange lockers. Smells from the cafeteria, mostly the starchy lingering of rice pilaf, hovered between him and Bruno as they passed. A few straggling students who were grouping together for morning classes sifted through the hallways. The track team stretched out in the corridor by the gymnasium in preparation of their running. He'd always wanted to run track.

He was fast. Maybe the four hundred meter, but he never liked the athletes, even the less jock-like runners.

The boiler room was past the gymnasium, and inside, Harley felt jumpy around the creaking and hissing of the pipes. The bolts holding the archaic system's joints and limbs together frowned on him with a sinister stillness. He didn't trust them. At any moment they could become weak and shoot from their holdings toward him.

Despite her size, Bruno slid past the piping to the back where it was even darker and snapped on a desk lamp over the metal desk she used as an office. The surface of it was scattered with supply forms and work orders and checklists. Bruno pulled a clipboard from beneath a sandwich wrapped in foil and handed it to Harley. She slipped into a dark closet and pulled out a caddy armed with the essentials of a janitor's duties: a fifty-gallon trash can, large trash bags for the restrooms and small bags for the classrooms, yellow caution signs for wet floors, plastic gloves and disinfectant sprays, shavings for spills or vomit, and toilet paper and paper towels for the bathrooms. The checklist showed a map of the building on the bottom half of the paper. The east wing of the building was his. The first floor was the English wing. Above it, science. Bruno sat on her desk after pulling a pack of Pall Malls from the center drawer. Harley let his arm fall to his side. The clipboard slapped against his thigh and he turned his attention to Bruno who shot a long stream of smoke into the air.

"You smoke?" She offered him a cigarette and Harley took one. He swiped his Zippo from his pocket, lit his cigarette in one quick motion, and thanked her.

Her hands flipped through the mess of papers on her desk. Her breasts heaved between her arms with her movement and Harley watched them until she pulled a stack of employee forms and handed them to him.

"You can begin tomorrow?"

"Definitely."

"Good. Fill these out."

Harley left the interview with a twinge of curiosity and excitement. Except for the landscaping and chores he'd done at the boys' home, he'd never had a job, and never work that paid. He folded the employee forms Bruno gave him and slipped them into his back pocket. During his walk home, he surveyed the abandoned buildings as he passed them. Most first- and second-story windows on the larger buildings were boarded up, and Harley entertained himself with the idea of squatting in one of them. He liked the fact that there were no windows to look out of, that he could play hide and seek with the world outside and nobody would ever think to look for him there, in the darkness and still air of something ignored and unloved, like the closed, lifeless eyes of a corpse. The day was much hotter than when Harley had arrived at the interview. Sweat formed at his temples and the ridges on either side of his nose. Skin on the back of his neck and ears burned and by the time he'd reached the apartment, a short, twenty-minute walk, the burn had bitten into the tops of his ears.

FIFTEEN

The walk left Harley's mouth dry, and he could smell the soap he'd used that morning sweating out of his pores. He saw Maggie sunbathing on the back lawn and made his way over the wooden porch with short, quiet steps. The slow movement made it difficult for him to keep his balance, so he pressed his fingertips along the edge of the house, leaving a sweaty streak over the storm windows as he passed. Harley held the screen door as he inched open the main door and kept his eyes fixed on Maggie.

Her bathing suit was a lavender two piece. The contour of her body rolled over the towel like the soft swells of approaching waves—her heels, calves, and ass. The movement of her shoulder blades and elbows were sharp and fell quickly as she slipped the knot of her bathing suit loose. She cast the magazine aside, turned her head, and lay calm against the towel, motionless. Harley watched her from the kitchen window with the run of sweat still pushing from his temples.

A fly landed on the soft part of her knee which she scared by flexing her hamstring to bring her foot into the air. Dirt collected on the bottom of her feet and formed a heart with the arches when she brought the other into the air. She pinched her big toe between the toes of her other foot. Harley let out a short gasp. Sweat glistened along her spine. The smallness of her hips locked into her waist like the molded plastic of an action figure. Her toes were all perfect, the nails painted. Despite how tiny she was, there was a firm strength about her. Harley trembled with awe of how beautiful she was, and how much that beauty demanded his attention—how it filled and pushed the air from the room, how much it made him fear what he wanted to do to it.

Harley sucked in a slow breath through his nose and gripped the corner of the counter. The breath he'd taken in and held tickled against the back of his tongue waiting to be released, and when he did exhale, the breath came out as a soft growl. Tension sifted through his sternum and lowered itself just below his navel as Maggie rolled over, her abs twisting beneath her breasts. He rubbed his palms dry against his pant legs, the left pulled taught by his erection, and Harley ventured into the magic of his thoughts.

Harley's knees locked in surprise at the sound of Sean's voice behind him.

"What the fuck are you looking at?" Sean asked.

Harley moved around the table away from Sean and shuffled the employment papers in front of him. "I was looking for a pen."

"Through the window?" Sean moved across the kitchen and looked out at Maggie. "I see what you were looking at. Got the hots for mommy?"

"Fuck you, Sean. I was looking for a pen."

"I always thought you were a fucking weirdo, but this takes the cake. You were checking out your mom."

Harley smoothed out the folds of the papers. Sean pulled a pen from his pocket and tossed it onto the table.

"You know, Harley, your mom is pretty hot. I can't really blame you for checking her out."

Harley picked up the pen. "It's nice you have an opinion of something other than school lunch."

"Well, she's definitely not school lunch. She's more like..." Sean's mind pawed for something of comparison.

"Wow, really?" Harley asked. "Maybe when you move on to something other than happy meals you'll come up with a better metaphor."

"Whatever, freak. Your mother ever tell you how we met?"

"Was she your babysitter?"

"You should ask her sometime."

Sean moved toward the door and nudged Harley's elbow on the way past that forced him to grind a black slash over the forms he was filling out. Harley set the pen down and shot his hand into his pocket. He squeezed his Zippo.

Maggie swatted at a fly on her left shoulder with the back of her knuckles then turned the page of the magazine she'd taken from the break room at work. She lay on a towel outside her apartment. The sun was high, and the heat, uncommon for that early in May, made the glossy pages of the *Redbook* she was reading difficult to see. The sun needed little effort to paint a sheen of bronze over her body.

Maggie blinked sweat from her eyelids and saw the shadow behind the window when she looked over her shoulder. She smirked at the thought of Sean peering out at her then rotated her head to scan the backyard and make sure there weren't any kids making their way home or neighbors spying from behind the pines that bordered the yard. When she rolled over, she slid a hand over her stomach and across her bare breasts. There was a moment of disappointment when she didn't hear Sean tap on the glass or come onto the porch, so she slid her index fingers along the edge of her bathing suit and readjusted it over the crest of her ass, revealing the tight slit she wanted to feel him separate.

Several minutes later, footsteps moved over the gravel toward her and she turned her head when Sean blocked the sun from her eyes.

"How was your nap?"

"I'm not finished with it. Why don't you come in?"

"Already? I haven't been out here that long."

Sean glanced toward the window and kneeled down to

stroke his fingers down Maggie's calf. "You have all summer to play in the sun. Besides, you don't even need a tan. Your skin is so beautiful already."

"You're such a sweetheart." Maggie turned her face away from him. "Ten more minutes, okay?"

Sean ripped a tuft of grass and twisted it between his fingers. "Why are you turning away? Who are you trying to look good for anyway?"

"Nobody, Sean. What are you talking about?"

"You sure? Because you sure look good to Harley. He was in the window watching you."

Maggie opened her eyes to the sting of her sweat and pushed her cheek harder against the towel. A tight knot of embarrassment locked in her throat.

He tossed the grass at her ribs and stood. "Fuck it. I have to go."

Small stones in the grass pushed against her ribs and stomach. She curled the edge of the towel between her fingers and pushed herself to her knees bringing the towel with her to cover her torso. Ants patrolled over the straps of her top and the edges of the bent corner of the magazine where she left them in the grass and strode into the house.

She made her voice tense when she addressed Harley. "I thought you were at a job interview."

Harley stared into the swirls of the wooden print of the table. His expression was something she'd never seen in him. There was still the sinister smirk that he'd been wearing since he discovered the power he had over language and the discomfort he caused others with it, but his eyes were lost, baffled.

"You alright?" Maggie asked him, tightening the towel around her.

He nodded.

"You sure? You don't look alright. But what about me, Harley? Do I look alright to you?"

"I need some air," Harley said, and ducked away from her

out the door.

In the hours that the house was quiet, Maggie decided to make dinner for Sean's return home, an attempt to wane their bickering that would probably prove futile. The refrigerator offered her nothing promising. Condiments, hardened bread, milk, and butter. The cupboard offered even less promise. Saltines and some canned, French-style green beans. Maggie shut the cupboard gently and stood in the doorway of her room. She found her jeans and pulled out random bills that she'd stuffed in the pockets. Back in her closet, she searched the pockets of other garments. At the end of her search, and after she'd dressed to leave the house, she had nineteen dollars piled on her dresser in wads and crumples. As she was leaving, the mailman dropped envelopes in her box. She separated them and glanced over the envelope addressed to Harley.

SIXTEEN

An envelope from the boys' home with his name on it was taped to the door when Harley returned. A small corner of tape stuck to the window when he pulled it loose. The door was locked, so he checked the old hiding places for the spare key, but only came up with cobwebs and the mice chewed cardboard stuck to his fingers. Then he checked a few more places he thought might be clever places to hide a key—the dryer vent, under the large rocks that outlined the parking spaces, even beneath the trash bags in the garbage bins and he thought of Sean. Maggie must've given him the spare key. Why wouldn't she? Wasn't that the norm, a basic domestic partnering gesture? Another portion of weight on a key ring, space on the floor to drop his clothes, a place at the bathroom sink for a toothbrush.

An argument from the neighbors' erupted, their voices smashing through the screens of their apartment. Glass broke and children began to cry. A scream pelted through the air as a man inside went to the windows and tore the books away that were propping them open. They slammed and the yelling and crying was hushed.

Harley sat on the steps and tore the flap from the envelope. Inside he found a check from the boys' home made out to him for $972.98. Somehow, he'd forgotten about the menial allowance money he'd earned from working on the grounds of the home. He didn't expect them to send a check. Harley took a while to study the envelope. The typed letters of his name where the check read: *Pay to the Order of* gave him a sensation of immense joy. To Harley, who'd never had more than the toe of a sock full of change, nearly a thousand dollars could buy him a way out of Maggie's, a start of his own, a second chance. The bank the check was drawn on was quite a distance across town, but he'd make the walk. Harley slipped the check back into the envelope, folded it into thirds, and pushed it into his pocket.

The arches of his feet hurt by the time he reached the bank. The lobby was cool and gave him a chill when he walked in. The place was full of smiles. Even Harley noticed his in his reflection on one of the glass partitions. Perhaps money did that to people, Harley wondered, giving them hope before they realized money had bought them everything but what they needed.

"Can I help you, sir?" a woman's voice asked.

Harley turned to a woman. She wore a beige business suit. Her name tag was perfectly level, as were the line of her teeth. She had gold bracelets on each wrist, pearl earrings, and a gold pendant necklace half hidden beneath her shirt. Harley admired the grace of her posture, the evenness of her shoulders, the symmetry of her eyes.

"I'd like to get money for this." He pulled the check from his pocket.

The woman took his check. "Do you have an account with us?"

Harley shook his head. "I just want money."

"Do you have identification?"

Harley pulled his state ID, social security card, and birth certificate from another pocket and placed them on the counter.

"I only need the ID."

She told him to endorse the check and made an attempt to convince Harley to open an account. Harley refused with a simple *no* and the woman maintained her kind demeanor.

He kept his money folded into quarters in a fist pushed deep in his pocket. His palms sweat around the bills and he gripped them tighter, fearful that somehow they would slip from his grasp. There was a deliberate focus on the things he held in his pocket—identification, money, the Zippo. The money and the identification papers had never been relevant to him. All he ever really knew about who he was, was that he was Maggie's kid—the tormenting burden on the men she'd tried to keep in the house. There was never any money, none that he ever carried around with him. Harley wondered what people did with these tools that gave him a social definition, something for others to define him, a name someone else gave him. But now there was money. Something he could give to people to have things he didn't need or want. Harley stopped walking and faced the street. The front of every building offered a temporary depository for people. They inserted themselves into those envelopments and exchanged paper or swipes of plastic for products they bought for other people to notice them. Hardware, groceries, auto parts, carpet and flooring, electronics, clothing, music, books, coffee shops, hair salons, tattoo parlors, bars, surplus stores, jewelers, and restaurants. People weren't fit to live in houses. They needed to roam. They needed the illusion that they were self-sufficient, settled, successful, accomplished. They needed to expose their lifestyle to everyone else, invite them to their homes with all their things, the place that made them feel like an unopened gift to the world. Tires rolled over the pavement before him. There was freedom. Wheels. Yes, wheels. That's what he'd do with his money. He'd buy wheels.

Harley never noticed before that there were more car dealerships on his way home than convenience stores. He had a difficult time believing that people needed places to buy cars more than the places that sold cigarettes or scratch tickets or bottles of soda. The Ford and Dodge dealerships faced each other on either side of the street. Flags and wind-dummies slapped through the air. Cardboard signs were propped in open hoods advertising a sale. Certified pre-owned signs hung in both stores' windows and Harley wondered what that meant, how they could certify that somebody had owned the car before. The places seemed like circuses and he'd be buying a car from a clown.

A mile from home, by the little league baseball field, where the grass was browned and scorched by the sun and heat and lack of water, was a used car dealership. Harley walked between the cars at one of the dealerships. Buy here, pay here. A sign hung above the neon OPEN on the small building behind a row of eight cars. Different years, makes, and models. There was no organization for them or ascending order of vehicle size like the Ford and Dodge dealerships. The building was no bigger than Maggie's living room with white linen curtains pulled to either side of the picture window to the right of the door. He stood out there for a while looking over the cars for a price written somewhere. A man trotted out of the small building when Harley got to the third vehicle.

The man's lips curved and grew in the center of his round face. When the man descended the three steps toward him, Harley felt the urge to run. He froze, unable to determine what made him want to flee. The man fixed a loose button halfway down his shirt, a short-sleeve white Oxford with a fat red tie stuffed beneath the collar and tight against his chin like a spear had pierced his jowls. The man's forearms were covered in a dense black hair that stopped just past his wrists. There was a mustard stain on the cuff of his khakis and his shoes were scuffed. Green from cut grass wrapped over the toes like dried blood. Harley's hands tightened into harder fists when the man stopped a few feet from him at the rear of the vehicle.

"Looking for anything specific?" the man asked.

"Wheels," Harley answered.

The man chuckled. "We got wheels, my man, on every one of these vehicles. Maybe the question should be, what would you like to see yourself driving?"

"It depends on how expensive it is. None of these cars have prices on them."

"There's a good reason for that. My name's Eric." The man

extended his hand toward Harley.

Harley relaxed his right fist and shook Eric's hand. "Harley. What's the reason?"

"Reason for what?"

"Why your cars don't have prices on them."

"Oh. Right. Don't you worry about price. We have ways around price tags. Take a look around. Cars are a lot like women. Sometimes you take what you can get, but it's always better to have the one you want. What do you want to drive, Harley?"

Harley was troubled with Eric's analogy, that people were possessions. A woman, like a car, was something temporary, something to get use out of until another was more affordable or appealing.

"I like the ones I can afford. Cars, not women."

"It could certainly apply to both. Well, let's take a look over here." Eric pivoted to Harley's left and touched his shoulder.

Harley glared at Eric's hand. Always touching. He'd heard that it was a sign of trust, touching. Letting another person slip parts of their body into your space like they were making sure you were there and not part of their imagination. They wanted you to trust them, but at the same time they either didn't trust themselves, didn't believe you, or both. Eric guided him around the cars to the white Audi parked on the grass on the corner of the lot. The car glistened in the sunlight, alone like a rare animal attraction at a zoo demanding the most attention.

"Now this baby suits you." Eric shuffled to the driver's door and opened it.

Harley detested the cleanness of the vehicle. It looked too new, like all the things that never belonged to him. All of its pieces were in place. There were no marks or visible damage. The signs of use were absent, and it created a feeling of uneasiness for Harley—a temptation that promised superficial benefits.

"I hate it," Harley said.

Eric tightened his lips over his gums in an attempt to maintain his smile. Harley noticed his efforts and felt a brief twinge of disappointment as if his rejection had been personal to the man.

"Good thing we've got more than one car." He led Harley to another car.

Again, Harley rejected it. And again at the next. And again. At the fourth car, an older model Buick with small patches of painted rust over the wheel wells, Eric leaned against the driver's door. His enthusiasm was gone and his smile had waned to a smirk.

"How much?" Harley asked.

"Fifteen hundred, and I'll throw in a full tank of gas."

Harley tightened his grip around the money in his pocket. "That's too much."

"Well, how much are you looking to spend?"

Harley thought briefly. "Five hundred."

Eric began to shake his head but faked a cramp in his neck and rubbed it out. "The only thing I can sell you is that." He pointed to the side of the building. A primer gray Ford Maverick with a busted grill and a large oval dent in the front quarter panel.

Harley marched to the car. He ran his fingers down the length of the body. It was gritty, textured, but resistant to the smudges the streets and the world would make attempts to leave on it. It had already suffered enough—like an old animal left behind the pack. Eric walked lethargically toward Harley and the car. He noticed Harley's excitement.

"Man," he whispered to himself. "Why would anyone want a piece of shit like this?"

That was the choice Harley made, had always made. The broken toys he'd swipe from piles of garbage on trash day, the partly used school supplies left in heaps at the end of the school year, the clothes he stole from the lost and found always found a home with him. He'd always found enough joy in having the things that nobody wanted.

SEVENTEEN

Maggie flicked her cigarette toward the bumper of her car. It hit a patch of rust on the corner of the trunk and the cherry died in a blossoming firework. She leaned back on the steps tapping her thumbnail against the head of a screw that had risen through the floorboards of the porch. A string of clouds floated through the blue sky like weathered fringe.

"Where the fuck is he?" she muttered.

The dinner that she'd prepared had gone cold, shake and bake chicken with boxed au gratin potatoes. Canned cranberry sauce and a platter of saltines doused with easy cheese. There was a chocolate crème pie in the freezer, which she felt like digging into.

Maggie pulled the pack of cigarettes from the step where she'd placed them next to her foot. She shook one from the pack and lit it and slapped the lighter on the wood beside her. Another drag, one that was harder to pull and seemed to bubble against her tongue. The cigarette paper was damp with blood at the edge of the filter. Semi-coagulated blood clung to the edges of her thumbnail. The Phillips head fitting in the screw protruding slightly from the wood was crested with blood as well, and Maggie stared at her thumb with bewilderment at the absence of pain. She cast the cigarette to the ground and lit another with her opposite hand, careful to avoid contaminating the paper.

Something large or heavy fell in the neighbor's apartment that jarred the abnormal quiet haunting the air. The thud rattled the loose windowpanes. Heavy footsteps moved through the interior next door. Then faster footsteps, more urgent. A man's voice called for someone. Mary? Erin? She couldn't tell. Softer footsteps, and then the shriek.

Maggie jerked, dropped the cigarette and the lighter, and looked toward the noise. It was not the sound of an uncomfortable infant or the wail of a child experiencing those first winces of pain. It was not the whine of annoyance or the yelp of fright. It was the sound of such distinct distress that it demanded nothing more than curiosity, more wonder than her phantom thumb wound. It was a scream of absurd realization—a scream of complete and total loss.

The neighbor, the man, stumbled through the door and fell over the stairs. The cement walkway lacerated his forearms and the palms of his hands. Maggie pushed herself from her seated position. He staggered toward her with his hands cupped upward. Blood from the cuts on his palms fell in small drops from the thin tendon between his fingers.

"My baby," he sobbed. "My baby is dead."

Sunlight wrapped itself around the string of spit stretching between the man's lips and strangled what was left of the moisture in his mouth. He fell to his knees and slumped forward. His bloody palms slapped over the back of his head. Blood hit the dirt and grayed in the dust. The man fell forward and sobbed into the dirt. At the doorway of the neighbor's house, a woman, his wife, waved her free arm into the air. She pressed a phone into her cheek with the other forming a white rectangle in the reddening flesh. Sweat matted her light brown hair against her face and strands clung to the phone as she pulled it from her ear and cast it away. The phone toppled through the driveway toward the street. Two children drifted behind the woman. It was the first time Maggie had ever seen them and not heard them.

The man continued to gasp and flattened himself against the dirt and small rocks and spit and cigarette butts and bird shit and small pieces of trash. Pieces of sand clung to his lips and teeth, at the corners of his eyes where it had rolled up his spouting tears. Maggie looked down at her cigarette that she was sure would be burning her fingers at any moment, but barely any of it had burned. The cigarette was burning away like the slow movement of traffic past an accident.

Garbled words rose from the ground. For a moment, it seemed like something hopeful, déjà vu, or a memory from her past she couldn't quite remember, a wish forgotten as quickly as the shooting star that inspired it. Harley came to mind. She wondered where he was, how fortunate, lucky, relieving—relieving, yes, how relieving it was that Harley wasn't there to witness.

Harley felt safe inside the car. He'd waited almost two hours for the dealer to help him process the insurance paperwork then make the trip to the DMV for the plates. After that, he tried his best to remember what he'd learned in driver's education at the boys' home. He never thought he'd drive his own vehicle. The world passed by him as he drove through the town, cutting down side streets and through the rich neighborhoods where everything from the shutters to the landscaped lawns and flowerbeds met at right angles.

Cars were aligned perfectly in front of garage doors, and wooden fences stood plum and sturdy. Even the colors were brighter, and Harley wondered where exactly the dingy, drab upholstery of the town bordered the Technicolor hues of the place he'd wandered into. He passed garden-gloved women on their hands and knees sifting through the dirt in their flowerbeds, landscapers lost in the drone of their mowers and leaf blowers, and a little girl riding her small pink bike—tassels wafting from the ends of the handlebars like a shocked, incredulous wave. The Maverick jerked through their streets like a rogue piece of toilet paper stuck to a shoe. People stared at him from where they stood in driveways or lawns or porches. Their glares spilled through his open window and Harley wondered if he was supposed to feel shame. It was almost as if they wanted to ask how he dared to move through *their* streets. Harley rolled up his window, a barrier of glass that kept him from the taint of the world he was driving through. As quickly as the colors had come, they drifted and Harley drove without destination back into the bleak, somber dishevelment of the town he knew. When he was deep enough in the gloomier neighborhoods and streets, and he could get his bearings, Harley drove back to Maggie's.

An ambulance rushed toward Harley in his rearview. He was only a few houses from Maggie's and it occurred to him, while he was pulling to the side of the road, that he hadn't thought about where or if he would be able to park his new wheels in Maggie's yard. A police cruiser sped down the street from the opposite direction and Harley noticed the neighbor. She stepped over the drainage cover in the street and waved with a beleaguered excitement, like a child who knows the music of an ice cream truck. The cruiser and the ambulance stopped simultaneously in front of the driveway to the neighbors' home and Harley turned his car off.

Paramedics rushed from the ambulance and ushered the woman toward her apartment. Harley paused a few steps from the yellow lines. The woman's face looked as though it'd been slapped repeatedly until the handprints had overlapped so much there was no indication that a hand had slapped her at all. It was the brightest red that Harley had ever seen anyone's face, and he assumed the paramedics had arrived in time to save whatever was about to kill her. Harley finished crossing the street wondering what might have happened to her, if her husband had lived up to one of his violent promises, until he saw Maggie in the driveway standing over the husband.

The man was shirtless. His elbows and hands were caked in what Harley thought was mud at first, but he found a few rogue blotches of blood and became even more interested in what might have happened between him and his wife. Maggie held a hand just above her stomach. She ignored him or didn't notice him, and she wasn't paying any attention to the man growling into the earth with his face and body smeared with blood and dirt. The man who'd made his children cry in similar fashion was mimicking them. Harley wanted to ask what happened, would have, actually, had the man's sobbing, what seemed like chortles, beckoned another curiosity in him. The man was not in any phase of toddler temper tantrum. There was so much pain. The man looked up at him, between sobs and whimpers, the slight natural gloss over the eyes was dull, like it'd been sucked dry. It was the most obvious look of despair and horror he'd ever seen—a look expressing the most savage agony, and the realization of the most profound lack of mercy. Harley stood beside Maggie and glanced at her face, her eyes fixed somewhere in the clouds.

"His baby's dead," she muttered and went inside.

Cops and emergency workers formed an indifferent gaggle on the lawn of the neighbors' home. Tragedy, it seemed, or waiting for it, beckoned chaos, as if the death was the balance in the order of the world. Order is what gave people their expectations of fairness and justification, but ask them to justify the death of a child and the best explanation anyone can offer is that God called his child to heaven.

When the cops finally organized themselves, and after a brief dialogue within their small group of who would be the two chosen to pull the grieving father from tear- and blood-soaked dirt, the officers made their way to the neighbor. The female struggled with helping the neighbor to his feet, and a younger male officer who seemed particularly annoyed or bored with his current task, escorted the man back toward his home. The world ends every day for someone, and one day the world would end for the neighbor and Maggie and Harley and Maggie's baby, just like it just had for the baby next door.

The table was set with plates of food when Harley went inside. Heat from the oven lingered in the kitchen. Harley stopped at the table. The smell of the food, set out for some occasion that he might have ruined for Maggie had it not been for the neighbor, tightened his throat. He scratched at the money in his pocket and realized he'd hand what was left over to her for a bite, for a memory of a meal or a set table or even that Maggie had ever put any effort into providing a meal for him.

"Help yourself, Harley. Nobody else is going to eat it."

She said it with such passive disgust that Harley ignored it. He started with the potatoes and barely noticed when she walked into her room.

PART TWO

EIGHTEEN

The neighborhood was quiet, and Harley basked in those moments sitting on the hood of his car and tracing lines around the clouds that passed above him in the evenings after work. More intense heat plagued the waning days of spring. Hope for comfort had evaporated in the hot, dry air. Maggie and Sean were spending more time bickering than usual, and Harley thought it was ridiculous that Maggie would even entertain any of Sean's thoughts or desires. The child's death next door had reduced the noise in the neighborhood to whispers. Even the other children didn't play outside as much.

Harley got used to his routine at work within just a few days. The work was boring and tedious, and the only excitement for Harley was trying to push a sloshing mop bucket through a hallway full of teenagers slamming lockers and rushing to their classes. It was like being stuck in the mud—never really gaining much ground, a few steps forward or back, and avoiding the feet kicking at the bucket. He kept his head down and spoke only to Bruno. Sometimes, he saw himself in smaller boys being pulled behind a staircase or their books snatched and dropped out of second-story windows.

A wheel on the mop bucket creaked as Harley pushed it through the science wing back to the janitor's closet. The workday over, Harley was anxious to get out. Students pulled books from their lockers for their last class of the day. The hallways began to clear except for two boys clustered near a set of lockers at the end of the hall. A girl struggled with her bookbag between them. The delicate contour of her eye sockets sloped into the bridge of her nose. Puffy red lips, pale cheeks, and thin eyebrows that curved above her eyes made her look almost doll-like, but not the doll-like way that those little girls they put in beauty pageants with their faces smeared in makeup that made them resemble a blow-up sex doll. Her hair was oil black and sleek and neatly pinned behind her ears. One of the boys moved and Harley saw that she had been struggling because there was a huge bulge in her belly where she held her bag and tried to zip it closed. Chants from the abortion picketers hummed in his ears. Harley pushed the bucket into the closet, catching the name of one of the boys embroidered in cursive on his letterman jacket, *Ricky*.

"How much dick are you going to suck this week?" Ricky said to the girl.

"If it's anyone but yours, Ricky, I'd at least be able to call it a dick."

Ricky slammed her locker closed. A metal clatter echoed down the empty hallway. A classroom door opened, and Mr. Reed came out. Reed taught earth science and had always taken interest in Harley when his other teachers didn't. Harley never understood why. Reed was thin, spending his afternoons running around the pond east of town during the months he wasn't coaching the boys' cross-country team. Harley listened from behind the closet door not wanting to embarrass himself by allowing Reed to see that one of his former students was now reduced to mopping and emptying trash cans.

"Don't you boys have somewhere to be?" Reed asked.

"We were just helping preggers here get her books into her locker."

"You're late for class. Get moving."

The boys walked past the door. "Later, cum-dumpster," Ricky whispered.

Ricky and his friend disappeared around the corner. Harley locked the closet and moved over to the girl after Reed went back into his classroom.

"Hey," he said, startling the girl and making her drop her bag.

Harley pulled the bag from the floor by the tote strap and held it out for her with the tips of his fingers. "Sorry," he said.

Her eyes slickened. "Thank you." The girl took the bag and turned her face.

"No problem. It's not that heavy."

She gave Harley one quick shot of her eyes. They were the color of sand, a light brown with a band of orange close to the pupil.

"Do you want me to walk you to your next class?" he asked as she moved past him.

"No. I have early release. I'm leaving."

Harley made a few quick steps after her. "Do you have a ride?"

"No." She stopped and adjusted the straps over her shoulders. "Why?"

"I can give you one."

"I don't take rides from strangers. Sex crimes, strangulation, those sorts of dangers, you know?"

"I'm not a stranger. I'm the janitor."

"I can see that." She tapped the embroidered name on his chest. "Harley. Cute name. Not Harley Remick by chance, are you?"

"Actually, yeah. How—"

"We started freshman year together. Then I dropped out for a while."

"I dropped out, too. I needed a luxury vacation to juvy."

"You're quite the smartass, Harley. I live down on Bates Street. Do you know where that is?"

"The Projects?"

"Yeah. The Projects."

"No problem. I'm parked behind the school."

The floorboards of his car were loaded with soda cans and crumpled foil from hot dogs. Harley managed, at least, to push the smut mags under the seat before she got in but missed the one face down on the dashboard. The girl swept the magazine up.

"That's not mine," he said.

"Sure." She looked at him. "What do you do with this? Get a little palm action before going in to mop the floors?"

Harley looked away from her.

"Don't get embarrassed. Every guy jerks off." She flipped through the pages, closed the magazine, and threw it back on the dash. She looked out the window and muttered, "And every guy's a jerk off."

"So how pregnant are you?"

"Seven months."

"Is that a lot of months?"

"Are you being serious?"

"No. I'm just not very smart. That's why I'm a janitor."

"You seem a little young to be a janitor."

"You seem a little young to be pregnant."

The smile dropped from her face like someone had kicked it off. "Yeah, well, whatever." She turned back to the window.

The intersection of North Avenue and High Street marked the center of low-income housing—the darkest section of the drab neighborhood, just past North Avenue. Harley had spent the first few years of his life in similar apartments on River Bank Court with friends of Maggie's who were only friends when they would babysit Harley. People called it *River Skank* because of the single mothers who populated it. He pulled onto Bates Street and stopped in front of her building. Rows of brick buildings lined the frost-heaved streets like destitution compounds. The streets were named for Ivy League schools—Yale, Harvard, Brown, Penn, Cornell, Dartmouth, Princeton, Columbia. She got out of his car without anything more than a *thank you* as she pulled on the handle. It didn't occur to him that he'd forgotten to ask her the obvious question until after she went inside. Her name.

She was locking the deadbolt when he got to the door and knocked.

"What?" she asked opening the door. "I don't put out, if that's what you're thinking."

"I don't know your name."

"Emily."

"My name's Ha—"

"Freshman year, remember?"

"Actually, I don't. How'd you even recognize me?"

"I didn't, honestly. The only person I know of named Harley torched my second-cousin's motorcycle."

"Shit. Small town, hunh."

"He's a fucking loser. I wish you'd lit him on fire, too."

"Can't say I didn't think about it."

"Do you want to come in?" she asked.

He walked in without answering. She sat him on the pale white couch and made coffee. The couch had a large brown stain over the arm rest and looked like something that had been dragged from the curb.

"Did you find this couch on the sidewalk?" Harley asked.

"Boy...aren't you just full of interesting observations. By interesting, I mean rude."

Harley apologized.

"Coffee?" she asked. "There isn't much else to drink here."

"Sure."

Coffee was a drink that he wasn't particularly fond of, but one that he enjoyed while she sat next to him. It was strong and bitter despite the three sugars she'd put in it for him. He wanted more sugar, but after she sat down, he didn't want to ask her for more. They each remained silent until Harley finished, put the empty cup in the sink, and went back to the couch. She had both of her hands resting on her stomach and she rocked the back of her head on the couch. She looked over at Harley.

"I really appreciate you giving me a ride, though it's weird I took one from you."

"Who is Ricky?"

"My ex-boyfriend."

"Is he the father?" Harley shot a finger toward her stomach.

"He doesn't want to be, and now he doesn't want to believe he is."

"Why wouldn't he?"

"He thinks I slept with someone else."

"Did you?"

"No." She sighed. "I can't believe that puny dick bastard got me pregnant."

"At least you know who the father is. My mother doesn't even know who mine is."

"Did you ever ask her?"

"Yeah, once, sort of. I was around eight or nine, and I asked her if I looked like my dad. She just started crying and locked herself in her room."

"That's fucking horrible. I'm sorry."

"It's probably for the better. My father would probably be some asshole like Ricky."

"That's likely. Most fathers are."

She began rubbing her stomach, the bulge, and Harley couldn't help but become curious as her hand moved in a small circle. The sight of a pregnant woman wasn't something he could easily pull from his memory, not a woman he'd seen up close, anyway. Emily's hand was cold when he grazed the pads of his fingers between her knuckles. She closed her eyes and kept rubbing.

"What are you doing?" she asked.

"I think I like you."

"No, you don't. You just think I'm easy because I'm pregnant. And you're also being a little fucking creepy."

"Does that mean you like me too?"

"Funny. Look, it's weird that I let you give me a ride. Part of it is that I haven't taken a shit in four days and the walk would have been unbearable. My mother's on her way now and I don't think you should be here when she gets home."

NINETEEN

Sean and Maggie were on the couch when Harley arrived home. Harley stayed in the kitchen and thought about Emily. He wanted to go back there, to her place. The only knowledge he had about interactions with women were what he'd learned from the stories other boys told in placement. From their perspective, every woman was a dumping ground not only for the boys' bodily fluids, but the baggage from their previous sexual encounter. Every woman was compared to the others, and those comparisons were always some form of degrading description of what they'd done that somehow validated their existence. They would just as easily talk about fucking someone's sister as they would fight if someone talked about theirs. And in all their explanations, Harley never heard how they approached women. It seemed that every sexual encounter he heard about started just before penetration. Even the magazines didn't help. The encounters were the same there, too.

He remembered his first erection, a night he wandered through the house to Maggie's room. He was very young. His shoulder poked through the neck of his oversized T-shirt. The door of her bedroom was open and the candles burning on her nightstands cast shadows against the walls. Maggie let out sudden shudders of breath until finally he could see her on the bed and the man thrusting behind her. Her jeans were bunched around her left leg, between her knee and ankle, and the other pant leg lay flaccid over the edge of the mattress. Her breasts swung in circles smashing against each other and the man slid his palm up her back and tangled her hair between his fingers. He jerked Maggie's head back and held it there. A vein throbbed in his flexed bicep and Maggie's face tightened. She let out a bursting moan and a smile twisted into her lips. She opened her eyes and looked at Harley. To the rhythm of the man's torso slapping against her, Harley's toes waved up and down against the cold metal strip across her doorway.

It wasn't much of a weight then, just a tiny tug against the fabric of his T-shirt. Harley pushed his hands down the fabric over his thighs. The small peak in the T-shirt was obvious, and he looked down at it wondering if it were that that caused the quivering low in his stomach. She was biting her lip when he looked back at her. She cupped a breast in her hand and pinched her nipple. She looked back at the man and said, "Come on baby, come. My kid's awake."

Harley was still thinking about Emily and how craving a kiss from her felt like the need for something sweet when Sean came into the kitchen and grabbed a Coke from the fridge.

"I heard you left school with that slut Emily Jensen."

"She's not a slut."

"She's slept with over twenty guys."

"So has my mother."

"You need to watch your mouth."

"I can't, my nose is in the way."

"Jesus, dude, really? Cute comeback. Sounds like something someone who lived with their mom would say."

Then he laughed. It was more of a repeated gasp—the sound of someone trying to breathe through a plastic bag. Harley reached into his pocket and flipped open the Zippo. He closed his eyes to the sound of Sean's gasp and thought of him engulfed in flames gulping for air in a panic as hysterical as his laugh.

TWENTY

Harley found Emily's schedule in the office while he was collecting the trash and waited outside of her first class. As he waited, he felt tremors through his body and his tongue retreated to the bottom of his mouth as he thought of what he would say when he saw her. The bell rang. Students filed from the classrooms and filled the halls, some of them tossing returned homework or papers into his bin that they had crumpled into balls. Harley kept his face down and pretended to rummage through his caddy as they passed. As each of them shifted into the chaos of the hallway, Harley's heart rate increased until there weren't any more students coming out of the room he expected Emily to be in. He checked the room hoping she would be shuffling from the back after struggling with her books, but he only met the curious look of a teacher. Harley grabbed the trash can at the corner and dumped it into the large bin in his caddy. The teacher smiled and went back to her notes.

Harley waited again at Emily's next class, that time with more curiosity, leaning into the row of exiting students, peering between elbows and over shoulders. Again, no Emily. He spent the rest of the morning immersed in his usual patrol, thumbing black smears from the hallway floors that cheap sneakers left with the scramble of foot traffic and taking graffiti off the bathroom stalls with brass polish, a trick that Bruno had showed him.

During lunch he cut through the cafeteria in hopes that he

would spot her, that maybe she'd arrived late, but he didn't find her there either. Ricky and the boy that had harassed her the day before sat at a round table in the corner. Harley met Ricky's glare with a stare of his own and a snicker. Trouble was coming. Trouble was always easy for Harley to find.

After he passed through the cafeteria, Harley made his way back to the bathrooms. Harley wrung the mop out and swatted the floor with its dirty tendrils. Ricky and his friend entered the bathroom and stood shoulder to shoulder. Ricky's friend held his stomach and grimaced.

"I didn't know it was a janitor's job to give pregnant chicks a ride home," Ricky said.

Harley tightened his grip on the mop. "That was strictly a volunteer effort."

"Maybe you should volunteer to let preggers make her own way home."

"Well, Ricky. The payment is a little too sweet to let her walk."

"Ricky, man. My stomach is killing me," the friend said.

"Don't be a pussy. Hang on," Ricky responded. "I'm not kidding around with you, mop bitch. You need to learn to mind your own business or that mop will be somewhere it doesn't belong."

Before Harley could respond, Ricky back-handed his friend in the stomach. The boy heaved, stuck his finger in his mouth and hurled a spray of foamy white liquid onto the floor. Ricky's friend quickly recovered and wiped his mouth with his sleeve. Ricky hocked and spat phlegm against the mirror.

"Have fun mopping, motherfucker."

Harley sat against the heater and flicked his Zippo open, trying to burn away the smell of vomit in the air. He thought back to his first major point of ridicule from his peers. Back in junior high when he puked in the aisle on the bus. Maggie had left a jug of expired milk and a box of mini wheats on the table for his breakfast before she left for work. The amount of sugar Harley dumped on his cereal that morning prevented him from tasting how sour the milk was. His stomach began to churn as the bus rolled up to the corner where he waited, and it was too late for him to run home. Halfway to school, Harley dropped over the seat and yacked, clearing other students to either end of the bus and forcing the driver to pull to the side of the road and move back to where Harley was still hunched over, his tears dropping into the pool of vomit.

"Goddammit, kid," the driver'd said. "You couldn't wait two more minutes. Clean this shit up." The driver tossed a roll of paper towels and a plastic bag onto the seat next to him. Vomit-muncher became a nickname constantly flung at him when he stepped onto the bus each day after that. Students refused to sit with him, or even less than two seats away, sometimes sitting three to a seat. It was then that Harley stopped trying to make friends. After that, he faded as much as possible against the walls and lockers, in the back of the classroom, shortcuts through the woods home, avoiding the streets and other students. He pursued nothing extracurricular except the solitude and echoes inside his bedroom. When he was forced to interact with other students, he found ways to irritate and annoy people. They were going to hate and ridicule him anyway. The least he could do was provide a reason.

Harley had finished his work early for the day even with the added cleanup of Ricky's addition to his duties. He waited in the boiler room to punch out thinking of his short drive home and how much he wished he didn't have to witness Maggie and Sean's engagement with each other. Like all of Maggie's relationships that he'd seen, there was a childish giddiness with her that wore off, and Harley would wait patiently for Maggie to extend some attention to him, which never came. She'd sulk in her room or bury herself in snacks on the couch and watch endless reruns of *Passions*. Maggie was approaching that stage of her relationship with Sean.

All of Maggie's relationships seemed like a distraction, at best, from the misery that she blamed him for, because he reminded her of his father. Sometimes, when Maggie was pissed about some new boyfriend, she'd go out and come home with a new one. He remembered those nights. Winter nights when they'd run out of oil and Harley would come home from school and the house would be cold with frost on the insides of the windows. He learned how to cook TV dinners by the time he was eight then he'd huddle close to the open stove to be warm as he ate mashed potatoes that were like tasteless cream of wheat and a fruit dessert that was always burned, even if the rest of the dinner was cold.

He sat in his car thinking of Ricky, how flammable the gel in his hair was, how his face would look if he doused his skull with flames. Coming through that image was Emily's face, the grittiness of her voice. The Maverick sputtered when he started it, but the engine rolled into its typical rumble, and he drove toward Emily's.

There was a trash bag outside her door that smelled like coffee grounds and something that had spoiled, fruit or rotting leftovers. Emily opened the door before he could knock. She was in a robe. Harley expected her to be sick, lips red from rawness and a pale face, maybe even a box of tissues in her hands. Behind her there was a small child in training pants pushing a toy fire truck into a wall of plastic cups. The truck had only three wheels and scraped against the floor where the fourth wheel was missing. Spit flew off his lips as he imitated the roar of an engine.

"What are you doing here?" she asked.

"You weren't in school today," he squeaked.

"Yeah. Joey was sick. He couldn't go to daycare."

"If that's Joey, he looks fine to me." He pointed past Emily's hip at the child who jammed his finger into the chassis knowing there was something wrong with the toy but not exactly what it was.

Emily rolled her eyes. "Yeah, well you know how kids can be. One minute they're fine, the next, running a fever and crying."

"I guess."

In her robe, Harley couldn't tell she was pregnant. Maybe because she was so small. The child looked a lot like her—same glisten to his eyes beneath dark eyebrows.

"Is that your little brother?"

"He's my son."

"Your son? You have a son, and you're pregnant?"

"What's that supposed to mean?"

"That didn't come out right. I just mean, well, you're so young. I didn't know you had a kid. I really didn't mean for it to sound like that."

She crossed her arms. Harley's left eye began to twitch, one of the signals he was nervous. He would have sat there all afternoon staring at her with his eye twitching if she hadn't said anything.

"Are you going to tell me why you came by?"

He shook the twitch away. "I didn't see you in school. I was worried."

"I don't need anyone to worry about me."

Harley looked down wondering what to say next, what he could say to sit next to her on the couch again. She was wearing multicolored socks with toes on them. The colors reminded him of Halloween, or fall. He could smell dead leaves and chocolate. The child made his way to the door and reached for her elbow with both hands.

"Muh-muh, I want a *soory*," the child said.

Emily took the child's hands in hers. "Okay, baby. Go play with your truck. I'll tell you a story in a minute."

"Muh-muh, who's that?" The child pointed at Harley with one hand and kept his focus on his mother. He moved his hand back to hers.

"This is a person who has a hard time understanding boundaries."

The child looked at Harley's hands, made a fish face and spit noises through his teeth.

"Okay, Joey. Go play for a minute."

The child returned to his fire truck and made more engine noises.

"He makes a lot of noise for such a little fucker."

"*Fucker*?" She made a loop around the straps of the robe with her thumb and finger and slid her hands down the sash.

"No, no, no. Not in a bad way. It's just an expression, that's all."

She reached for the door handle and began twisting it. "Look, I really have to get back to him. Maybe I'll see you in school."

"Can I come in? I mean, I want some coffee. No, I don't mean—can we hang out for a while?"

"I have to put Joey down for a nap and I'm in a bathrobe and I haven't showered today, I just—"

"Let me watch him while you take a shower then you can put him down for a nap and we can hang out."

"I don't know." She crossed her arms again and looked in on the child.

"Even if you put him down for a nap, you're still not going to be able to take a shower. This way, you don't have to worry about him eating anything bad or playing with the stove or sticking your keys in the electrical outlets."

"What kind of a hell kid does that?"

"My mother told me I did those things when I was a child."

"Your mother must be a wreck by now."

"Train wreck, maybe. So, what do you say?"

"Alright. But you can't teach him any bad words."

"No problem."

She motioned Harley in and shut the door behind them. Harley took a seat on the couch as Emily spoke to Joey. She kissed his forehead and Harley peered at the action, envious. Upstairs, her heels pounded back and forth against the floor a few times before the water came on. The child peered at Harley over his shoulder, mouth open and lips slick with saliva that was beginning to run down his chin. He breathed through his mouth into his belly. Fragile, pudgy fingers bent to what seemed like a point that they might snap against the floor. Harley wanted to speak to the child, but a topic of conversation with a child did not resonate in him. Harley found difficulty communicating with adults. How was he supposed to initiate conversation with a kid? Not even a kid, yet. Younger than a kid. Maggie was dating a kid. Joey was practically an infant.

TWENTY-ONE

Mr. Tobias was stacking a display with Table Talk Pies when Maggie got to work. Sweat marks showed under his arms and in a long, trough-like smear down his spine. The air conditioner hummed and growled directly above his head and blew air just past him. The hottest part of the store had to be right below that appliance. The corners of his mouth rose softly when she entered, and he pushed the bridge of his glasses up the sweaty slope of his nose. Maggie closed her eyes to avoid that interaction with him and made her way to the break room for her apron and a few final touches to her makeup. His footsteps followed behind her.

She had her back to the break room door when he entered, her fingers twisting the straps of her apron into a knot at the small of her back.

"Hey there, Mr. Tobias," Maggie said before she turned around.

"Hi there, Margo," Tobias replied, tamping away at the sweat on his forehead.

"Yes?"

"I was just going over the schedule for next week, and I was considering giving you a weekend off."

"But I didn't ask for a weekend off. Why would you—"

"Oh, well, you know, ah, see, uhm, I rented a cabin in Ithaca on Cayuga Lake next weekend and—"

"Are you asking me to spend the weekend with you?"

"Oh, gosh, no. Not the weekend. Just wanted to extend an invite for you if you wanted to, you know, spend some time on the lake while this weather is so dang intolerable."

"I have plans this weekend with my son. We've been counting down the days to this, so, I can't. Thank you, though, for the invitation. I really appreciate it."

Tobias wobbled his head and told her that he understood before leaving the break room.

Courtney was counting down the drawer when Maggie got to the front of the store. The other girls still called her *new girl* even though she'd been there for a year. There were even girls that were newer who called Courtney *new girl*. She didn't seem new to Maggie, but a familiar face that couldn't quite get the hang of things. Maggie watched her whisper her addition out loud and make small marks on a piece of receipt paper. A customer stepped into line and Courtney looked up at him trying to continue her count in her head, but she lost it. The tiny smile she'd given the customer, more the beg of mercy for his patience, vanished and she looked down at the money in her hands as if she'd just broken from a raging psychotic blackout to find a bloody murder weapon. Courtney slipped the money back into the drawers and began her count again.

Another customer joined the line, and the original customer looked at Maggie with the same plea for mercy that Courtney had given him. He was a slender man, his face tired and smeared with dirty sweat. His T-shirt, jeans, and boots were stained with grease. Maggie knew his look—the look of a man who spent an hour every morning trying to work the stiffness from his hands. Sweat built on the gallon jug of milk the man had resting on the conveyor next to Courtney. Immediately, she thought of Tobias sliding sweat from his face. A woman joined the line and Maggie wondered where the people were coming from. Nobody had entered the store since she'd been standing there. Sometimes, it seemed they hid in the shelves waiting for a moment like that, when it's so easy to turn a cashier's day into a shitshow, that they come from their hiding places and revel in the misery they cause. When the sixth customer joined the line, and was standing beneath the air conditioner, Maggie whispered to Courtney.

Tears welled in Courtney's eyes and the look of stress and discomfort was so marked on her face, that she seemed to have been struck by something large and heavy. Maggie maneuvered around the conveyor and placed a hand on her shoulder.

"What was your X-reading?" she asked.

Courtney trembled. "I can't get the balance right."

"Don't worry about the balance. What is your X?"

She looked at her receipt. Maggie winked and pulled the money from the drawer. "Take this and go count in the back. I'll take care of the over/under."

"But—"

"These people don't want to wait anymore. Tobias will be more pissed about that. Go ahead."

Maggie turned to the first customer and gave him a total before she'd scanned anything. The man's eyebrows rose with impression when the display proved her right.

"Do me a favor, stud," Maggie said as she took his money. "Drop that milk off in the cooler and get yourself another gallon on your way out."

The man made an attempt to smile, a learned response to kindness, but could barely separate his lips, so instead made his way on.

Maggie stood behind the conveyer, inflating with false interest and enthusiasm with each new customer. She swept the line through the store and the place had resumed its normal midafternoon lull with a few muffled sounds of customers moving up and down the aisle.

Courtney returned with her count from the drawer followed closely by Mr. Tobias whose disposition was marred by a look of frustration.

Courtney placed the small, paperclipped stack of bills on the conveyor before Maggie. "Thank you," she whispered. "Mr. Can't-Catch-His-Breath is pissed."

Maggie burst into laughter. The girl had hardly said anything to her before that moment. A few *excuse-me*'s and head nods had been the bulk of their interaction. Maggie didn't expect the jab at the boss, especially not one while he was just a few feet behind her.

Tobias twisted the ends of his fingers. "Maggie," he huffed. "We can't allow employees to wander through the store with large amounts of money, especially when their drawer has not been zeroed. This is exceptionally unexpected behavior on your part."

"There was a line forming pretty quickly. I didn't want the customers to have to wait."

His cheeks had begun to shed their redness. "Well, that's very good thinking on your part, paying close attention to the customer's needs, but it still leaves you responsible should the money count be off. Don't let this happen again. New G—" Mr. Tobias stopped himself. "Monique will simply have to keep her register open should a rush like that come in again if she's the only register open."

"Okay, Mr. Tobias. It won't happen again. Her name is Courtney, by the way."

"Oh, gosh. Thank you, Maggie. I hope I wasn't too hard on you. It's just that I can't afford to take any kind of loss. I certainly wouldn't want to lose you as an employee. You're good with the customers. They've even told me so."

"Thank you, Mr. Tobias. That's reassuring to me."

Tobias waddled away, and Maggie stuck a middle finger in the air at his back.

TWENTY-TWO

It took Harley several minutes of thought to engage Joey. He began with a few approaches, what he thought were reasonable attempts to vocally interact, but stopped himself before he allowed any sound to form in the air between them. Finally, with Joey's toys acting as prompts, Harley began to ask questions.

"Do you like race cars?" he asked.

The kid continued staring, frozen, waiting for his mother to comfort the situation.

"How about tractors? Spaceships?"

Joey picked his nose. Harley was humored, and tempted to coach him. After a while, the child pulled his finger from his nose dragging out a monstrous green slug that stretched from his square, uncut fingernail. Joey stared at it like it was a live creature that would squirm in his hand.

"You gonna eat that?"

Joey looked up the stairs for his mother. The water was still running. He looked back at his finger and scrambled to his feet, marching out to the kitchen. At the refrigerator, he looked back at Harley.

"Saving it for later? Good idea."

Joey smeared the booger across the refrigerator door then squatted to admire his work. Harley rolled into a chuckle, and Joey turned to him to scrunch his face. The fire truck skidded across the floor when Joey kicked it during his high-step charge toward it. That refrigerator door empty and bare of anything but a few alphabet magnets made Harley think about Joey's life. How he would grow, and perhaps eventually, the door would be decorated with popsicle stick projects and finger-paintings. Joey would discover paste and see other children eat it. Those were the kids that ate their own boogers. At least Joey had a chance at life.

Joey crashed his fire truck into the cups then rammed one cup, chasing it around the living room. When the cup was finally demolished, he left the fire truck on its side and tried to stand. He dropped once on his ass, making the other cups bounce slightly but managed to get to his feet again and pull a story book from a pile on the staircase. He pointed at the cover and looked at Harley.

"You want me to read you a story?"

Joey scrunched his face and made a terrible sound, relief, like he'd finished shitting himself. He brought the book to Harley and placed it on his lap. His finger was still pointing at the cover, a puppy. *The Pokey Little Puppy*. Harley remembered it from his own childhood. It was his favorite, the first book he'd learned how to read. He pulled Joey onto the couch, opened the book, and began reading.

Joey pointed at every picture and grumbled something. A couple of times he pushed the pages back that Harley had turned to point things out he thought Harley had missed. The child smelled like a sweaty, summer pillowcase that hadn't been washed in a long time. It almost distracted Harley from the story. He didn't remember the story being so stupid. As a child he was amazed by it, but that was also true about clowns and the ability to ride a bike without training wheels.

"*Puddy*," Joey said.

"Puppy."

Joey pointed at a puppy in the story. "*Puddy*," he said again.

"That's right. It's a puppy."

"*Puddy thit.*" Joey tapped his finger on the page.

"Puppy shit. Very good."

"*Puddy thit.*" Joey got louder.

"Maybe he already did."

"*Puddy thit!*"

"Yeah, you said that already. Let's try a new one."

The child slapped the book. "*Puddy thit!*"

"He already did. The puppy can't shit anymore. He's just a puppy."

"What did I tell you about teaching my kid bad words?" Emily asked. She stood at the top of the stairs with a towel wrapped around her head and another around her body. Her stomach showed and her collar bones were still damp.

"He said it. I didn't teach him."

The child looked up at Harley then back to his mother holding a finger on the edge of the book.

"He's saying, *puppy sit.*"

"Oh." Harley looked down at the child. "He's not listening to you, is he?"

Joey stared at his mother, open mouthed. She moved down the stairs and scooped him off the couch to pull him up on her shoulder. He wrapped his arms around her neck like a trained monkey.

"Say bye, bye," she said.

"Buh-bye."

She brought Joey upstairs. Her voice echoed down to the living room and Harley imagined her stacking stuffed animals around him, the child comforting himself with his thumb and curling up into the warmth below his blankets. But there were probably no stuffed animals. Harley'd never had any. He finished the story while he waited for Emily to come back down. There were only a few pages left. The pictures weren't getting any more captivating, so he finished it quickly and couldn't tell why he thought that story was so amazing when he was a child. He wondered if all his favorite childhood stories would seem stupid to him after so many years.

Emily returned wearing sweatpants and a Jets jersey. Even

though the clothes were baggy, the curves and slopes of her figure were still visible. She sat beside him on the couch, cross legged, and held her shins with both hands drumming her fingers against the bone.

"So, tell me, Mr. Janitor. What is it about me that had you so worried?"

"About what?"

She slid her arm over the back rest of the couch behind Harley. "That's why you came over here, right? You said you were worried."

"Yeah. Well, kind of." Harley wiped his fingers over the corners of his mouth.

"So what's the real reason? I already told you I'm not putting out."

"What if I paid you?"

"Excuse me?" Emily pulled her arm back and folded them over the jersey's numbers.

"It was a joke."

"I hope so."

"I don't even have any money."

"You're pretty funny." She relaxed her arms.

"I've been called a lot of things. Never funny though. That's a first."

"Please. Nobody has ever told you that you were funny?"

"Not really."

"What do people tell you?"

"They just give me dirty looks. That says enough without saying anything. When they do say something, it's usually, *fuck off.*"

"Maybe you hang around the wrong people." Emily pushed her hand over Harley's knee ."Do you have a girlfriend?"

"She doesn't like it when I call her that. But she doesn't like being locked in the closet either, so we've come to an understanding."

"What the fuck?"

"You jealous?"

"Of course. That's every girl's dream."

"Well, shit. If it's that easy, why have I never had a girl-friend?"

"You've never had a girlfriend."

Harley shook his head.

"Have you ever had sex?"

"I had a threesome once."

"Really?"

"My hands count, right?"

"Gross. Oooh." She squinted and put her palm against the lower part of her belly.

"What's wrong?"

"She's kicking. You want to feel?" Emily reached for his hand.

The palms of her hands were hot against his knuckles as she guided his quivering fingers to her stomach. Like relationships, an invitation to touch someone had never been extended either. He'd never been offered a handshake, a hug, or even a wave goodbye. The football jersey was cool, and his expectation of her belly being soft met him with surprise. It was firm, like a warped tire. A tingling sensation spread through his groin. A lump pushed into the center of his palm and he jerked his hand away.

"Jesus," she said. "It's not going to bite your damn hand off. Go ahead, feel it."

He pushed his hand beneath her jersey and felt the corrugated scars of her current pregnancy overlapping the scars from her previous one—long slashing parts of skin that grooved down toward her hips like a trail through sand. He touched them with delicacy then stretched his hand out and waited. Emily breathed in slow deep breaths, scouring his face with her gaze until he felt uneasy looking at her eyes. Her fingers pinched the top of his ear lobe. She didn't blink. When her fingers touched the base of his jaw, he closed his eyes. There was shifting on the couch, and her breath hit his lips.

Joey's feet thumped from his bed and they stopped. Emily pushed away from him and hurried upstairs. Her voice hummed through the rooms as she spoke to Joey. Harley stood when she returned, and she met him in the middle of the room. Her eyes jerked back and forth over his face and she asked him to leave.

TWENTY-THREE

June 1977

The first morning she threw up, Maggie was looking at one of the many pictures of her brother that her mother had posted throughout the house. Glossy, photogenic Post-it notes of his memory. Don't forget how much more Edith loved him. Above the sink was the eight-by-ten color photo of him squatting, wearing camouflage with a shotgun cradled in his arm and a line of geese at his feet. She wretched over the side of the table nearly falling from her chair. Edith stood and cradled her and ushered her into the bathroom.

"Must be that bug that's going around," she said. "Couple people at work called out with it."

Bug, Maggie thought. Yeah, that was it. A bug. It happened again the next morning, and the morning after that. The third morning, her mother came into the bathroom with a small cardboard box. She stood rigid glaring down at her daughter with her arms crossed and tapping the box against her shoulder.

"This is no bug," she said and held the box in Maggie's face. "Make sure you read the instructions."

Maggie shook her head at it, wishing the vomiting would return so she didn't have to take it.

"You take this and you do it. Pray you're not what I think you *are*."

She didn't need to take the pregnancy test to know what she *was*. The hours she'd spent at the library crying into the pages of pregnancy books had already made her sure. She didn't care what her mother thought she *was*. All she could care about—fear—was that she'd be forced to bear the weight of what was inside her crushing anything hopeful she had ever dreamed of or would ever dream of. She could never dream again of how a man would tell her he loved her before she gave her body to him, her flesh, for the first time.

Edith grabbed Maggie's arm. Her grip tighter than any man's she'd ever known. "You do this test and pray that God forgives your sinful ways."

"Get out," Maggie mumbled.

"Excuse me?"

Maggie turned her face from the toilet ready to scream the events into her mother's ears and watch her curdle into the oblivion the truth would create. But instead of words coming, she turned her head back to the toilet and continued with her sickness.

"I've been a good mother. My whole life I've done good by you and this is how God repays me. He took my son." Her mother stifled the start of her weeping.

"If only he had taken him sooner."

Edith slapped her face. "And Satan has taken my daughter."

With vomit coated on her lips, Maggie turned her stinging cheek to her mother. Tears crested the edge of her nose. "Get out, mother."

Edith set the box on the edge of the sink and left the bathroom. Maggie gripped the box, squeezed the cardboard around the stick inside, then sent it flying toward the door. "Take God with you," she cried.

Nurses had taken urine and blood samples and she was waiting in the small room staring at a poster diagramming the inner ear.

Cold paper spread over the exam table, as cold as the last words she'd had with her mother. Twice the nurse had to ask her to undress and put on the johnny. She wrapped her thumb around the cool metal of the stirrups where her feet would go and hoped the doctor would come in with good news, a second chance. After all, she deserved a second chance, a moment to feel relief. *Second chance.* She gripped the stirrups tighter with the thought of it, how she'd phrased the thought. *Second fucking chance?* A second chance only came if you'd had one in the first place.

When the doctor came in, she expected a look of scorn, for him to look at *mother's little sinner—the damaged little whore who couldn't keep her legs closed.* But he smiled and set the clipboard with her charts on the counter with the jars of tongue depressors, swabs, and cotton balls.

"Hello, Margaret." He pulled the wheeled stool from the corner and sat slapping his palms against his knees. "Well, you are pregnant."

She gripped the stirrups tighter and let her shoulders drop. *Second fucking chance.* Dr. Walsh waited for her to say something, but she stared at the swirling loop pattern on his maroon necktie. She listened to her thoughts, some of them echoing the harsh words of her mother, others dictating the end of youthful experiences. *No prom, no dress, no more gooey looks from the boys in the hallway, no white wedding, no cake, no birthday celebrations, no college, no youth, no hope, no second fucking chance.*

Walsh touched her wrist with the edge of his index finger. "Margaret, sweetheart, you need to let go." His voice startled her as if he'd appeared in the room unnoticed. She looked down at his hand. His fingers were cold, and thin. They were perfect, the fingernails cut and filed with a thin white crescent along the edge of them. "Margaret, I'm sure you want to get this over with as soon as possible. Lie back so I can take a look at you." He had his thumbs against the edge of her palms trying to peel them from the metal. She bit her lip and let go.

Despite his hands and fingers being slender, the size of them compared to hers made them brutish. She squeezed around his thumb, the way a small child grasps the hand of their parent when crossing the street, and dragged the tips of her small fingers against the paper. His other hand pressed against her back between her shoulder blades as she reclined squeezing her eyelids closed and clenching the muscles along her groin. When her back hit the paper and the cold, she tensed as if the cold had latched on and gotten a firm grip of her ribs. The doctor slid his hand from the small of her back and used it to pry his thumb from her grip.

He instructed Maggie to put her heels in the stirrups and guided her there when she finally moved them, each knee heavy with reluctance as she moved. One foot in the stirrup then the other. Cold metal biting at her ankles. Dr. Walsh scrubbed his hands at the sink. Water slurped at the drain. The stretching whine of the gloves over the doctor's hands as he forced his fingers into them. He positioned himself in front of her, between her legs. The wheels of the stool chirped. She reached up to grip and steady her knees.

"This will only take a few moments," he reassured her, fumbling with something shrouded by her johnny.

When his fingertips pressed against her leg, they lacked the texture she'd expected. They were lifeless, no temperature to them, smooth, anonymous. He warned her of the tension and then it was there, the instrument burrowing inside her, discovering the sin her mother accused her of. Maggie could see the expressionless form of his brow and the instrument retreated slowly with the rise of his eyebrows. His eyes came over the edge of her johnny, the skin of his cheekbones pulled tight by the parted expression of his lips. He set the instrument down and stood kicking the stool with his heel. The gloves snapped as he tore them from his hands and leaned against the counter over his charts.

"You can sit up," he mumbled.

Maggie pushed her strength to her abdomen, pulled her legs

from the stirrups, and sat up. There it was, the memory inside her, and the doctor wearing his taste of the horror on his face—the shocked, appalling expression like those that form after viewing atrocious pictures on the walls of museums or magazines.

"Who did this to you?"

Maggie squeezed her legs together and folded her arms across her stomach. "Did what?" She shook her head and did her best to keep the tears from coming.

"Margaret. There's vaginal scarring. The kind that happens when a woman is..." He took a slow breath. "Does your mother know? There are options. You don't need to go through with this."

"No. My mother would never."

"I think your mother might change her mind if she knew."

"That will only make it worse. She can't know."

"Well if you explain it to her—Margaret, this isn't your fault."

"She won't see it that way."

The doctor scribbled on her charts. "You can put your clothes on. I'll be back in a moment."

Maggie dressed and waited in the chair for the doctor to return. He came in a few moments later with her mother. Edith stood just inside the door and clutched the bible she always carried against her chest. Her lips moved, and Maggie could tell she was praying. Soft mumbled whispers to an imaginary friend. Walsh took a seat in the swivel chair between them.

"I think we should open up a dialogue about Margaret's future."

Edith clenched her eyes. "Are you pregnant, Margaret?"

"It's pretty obvious, isn't it?"

Dr. Walsh sighed. "There are options, Ms. Remick. Given Maggie's age and the circumstances, I think she might recover from this if the appropriate steps are taken. Do you have a family psychiatrist?"

The woman narrowed her eyes. "We are a family of God.

We don't condone head-shrinkers or voodoo who-do."

"Ma'am, based on my examination, I doubt Maggie will be able to carry the child to term. It would be a grievous experience for her, far more pain than any woman should bear, brutal, in fact, for her to continue the pregnancy."

"She got herself into this mess. She needs to accept responsibility."

"You're absolutely right, Ms. Remick, which is why I think terminating the pregnancy would be the best possible scenario for Margaret. Why force her to—"

"I'll hear nothing of the sort, Doctor. She'll not contribute to her sin by committing another."

"Ms. Remick, if Margaret carries this baby to term, it could kill her."

"Then perhaps she'll have a chance to be with God."

TWENTY-FOUR

Late Spring 1997

Harley compared the firmness of Emily's stomach to everything he touched on his way home—the head rest of the passenger's seat, his flexed thigh muscle, the contour of the dashboard, the back of his head, the fibrous texture of the plastic trash can wobbling in Maggie's driveway, the near empty container of milk from the fridge that he finished and left on the counter, the bubble of the television screen when he grabbed the remote, the armrest of the couch as he sat, even his own stomach as he pushed it out and searched for something on the TV. Maggie's stomach would look like Emily's soon.

Harley felt himself drawn to his mother's room. Not since he was a child had he wandered into her room, and then it was only to look for Christmas or birthday presents that were rarely there. Most gifts he received came in the thrift store plastic bags where Maggie'd bought them. In the closet there were a few shirts hanging that belonged to Sean, some dresses and other clothes hanging that Maggie only wore when she was single and heading to the bar. *ATV* magazines and *Soap Opera Digests* were meshed together on her dresser. Their underwear and clothes were intertwined in a laundry basket beneath the window. Next to that was a night light. The blanket and sheet on her bed were twisted together and draped over the corners. Harley wondered what it felt like to wake up on that bed, next to Maggie. Before he could inspect more of the room, keys hit the lock on the kitchen door. Harley bolted back into the living room.

Sean and Maggie came in laughing and continued to laugh as they entered their room and slammed the door. Maggie's giggles forced him from the apartment. Harley walked to the end of the block and turned right toward the city park behind the library. He cut through the park when he was younger. Sometimes in the winter, Harley would huddle beneath the slide and pack snow on either side of him to break the wind. Beneath the slide, he'd think of his favorite stories and imagine himself there, with the Swiss Family Robinson or on Treasure Island, only to crawl from the hideout at dark and walk home and over the planks of the porch to drown in the absence of compassion and humor and love. Harley sat at a picnic table by the basketball court and pulled a pile of pine needles from the ground.

A group of boys shot baskets while he lit the tips of single pine needles with his Zippo. Their bikes lay in a heap like grenade victims. They missed shots, threw air balls, and said *fuck* between every word. The streetlights were coming on. The cops would be at the park soon, rushing the kids out of there so they could find trouble stealing things from parked garages and cars. They might even go down to the mills and smash some windows, however few there were left.

The kids told dirty jokes and lied about what they did to their babysitter the last time they had one. One kid began talking about different things. He talked about his brother who was in the Army and was coming home for good. Then there was the list of all the things they were going to do together: go waterskiing out at Cayuga, chase girls on race day down in Watkins Glen, learn cool ways to kill people with their bare hands, and go down to Ithaca to bash faggots. Harley wondered if older brothers did those kinds of things. He'd heard about other older brothers that used their younger brothers for punching bags. Maggie'd had a brother, but Harley'd never met him. He'd only heard his grandmother talk about how much of a saint he was when she caught Harley misbehaving or when she criticized Maggie for something. Harley continued to burn needles and listen to the boys until they untangled their bikes and left. For a while after that, he stayed and listened to the sounds die out with the flickering blinks of sunlight disappearing through the leaves of the maples across the park.

Maggie was alone and lying on her couch in the dark when Harley returned to the apartment. He turned on the light to see that was not knowing she was crying. She put her palm in the air to block the light then rolled her face into the cushion. A similar scene. One that he'd seen so many times before.

"Are you okay?" he asked.

"Just leave me alone, Harley. I don't want to hear it tonight."

"What happened?"

"Harley, I'm serious. I'm not in the mood for your jokes or insults."

Maggie's tears were usually caused by the anger she felt at rejection, not sadness. He understood that about her, or at least he thought he did, because that was always the only thing that would make him cry.

"Tell me what's wrong." Harley sat on the couch at her feet.

"Why the fuck do you care? You just want to sit there and give me that smirk and say, *I told you so.*"

"What are you talking about?"

"Sean left."

"You told him about the baby?"

"No. I didn't tell him about the baby." Maggie sat up on the couch and balled her fists against her forehead.

"Then why did he leave?"

"Harley, don't pretend to care. You can't sit there and say you're not happy he's gone."

"Seeing you cry doesn't make me happy."

Maggie's hands hung limp as she pressed her forearms against her thighs. "Yeah? You want to know why he left? He left because of you."

"Because of me? What the fuck did I do? What, captain night light can't take a few jokes?"

"Right. Be a smart ass. You can never take anything seriously, can you?"

"What is there to take serious? I'm a fucking janitor. You're nailing a kid in high school. How am I supposed to take anything seriously?"

"Just leave me alone, Harley, please."

"Is that what you really want?"

"That's all I want right now."

Maggie stood and looked down at Harley. When Harley looked away from her, she walked quietly to her room. Harley waited for her to close her door before standing and going to his own room.

His sheets smelled like sweat from his dreams the night before—scenes of small dogs fighting. The smell, even though it was his own, forced him to roll to his back. Lying on his back made it harder to sleep, because it had always been harder to block the noise. When he woke in the middle of the night, he brought his frustration with Maggie with him, how he'd engaged her only to get even more rejection from her. He couldn't bear to be in the house anymore, to hear her whimpers seep through the walls and into his room. At the boys' home there had been function. He didn't have to pretend to like anyone or anything. There was simply routine and schedule, a process to learn some things that nobody had ever taken the time to teach him before. He slept in a bed that was more comfortable than the one he lay in while he thought of Maggie and her crying and the pain he caused her without ever really knowing how he'd caused it. There, with her, his function was the constant pursuit of comedy in the tragedy of her life. He got out of bed and went outside to sleep in his car. Air so dry and hot it was hard to breathe.

TWENTY-FIVE

The sunlight streaming through the back window woke him. He'd slept on his hand and it was numb. It felt swollen and tingled. Maggie and Sean's voices were behind him in the driveway. They stood outside the back door, hugging. Maggie held a bouquet against his back between his shoulder blades. When the embrace was over, Sean kissed her on the cheek and bounded down the driveway to the street. Harley wondered how someone could redeem themselves by giving someone something that was going to die. It was a morbid symbol of love—here's something that's pretty but will die very shortly. It made sense as long as the flowers kept arriving. Harley thought of Emily and wondered if anyone had ever given her flowers.

The woman at the flower shop stood behind a bouquet she was building, peering at Harley over her thin glasses—yellow and red and white petals hid the lower part of her face. There was a wall of cards that he perused, an assortment of rhyming poetic gibberish printed on them. Cards for everything—birth, death, wife, husband, birthday, mother's day, father's day, secretaries, congratulations, sympathy, get well—fuck off. Why didn't they have a card for that? If there was a card for everything else—the arbitrary emotions of joy or the pursuit of it, why weren't there any cards to describe how a person felt if they were miserable? Some people lived in horrible circumstances, and living was merely surviving. At the boys' home, they'd said Harley was depressed. They gave him pills—magic pills so he wouldn't be. Harley wasn't depressed. He was miserable, and depression is a state of joy compared to misery. Harley thought of a whole slew of cards for other special occasions— *hope you die soon, you're not invited, you're fired, fuck off.* Where were the fuck-off cards?

"Can I help you?" the woman asked.

"Fuck off."

She dropped her scissors. "Excuse me?"

"I was wondering why you don't have any *fuck-off* cards. You have everything else," Harley said, pointing down the aisle of cards.

The woman muffled a chuckle. "Oh. I thought you were telling me to—never mind. Why on earth would you want a card like that?"

"I don't. I was just wondering." Harley pulled a card from the shelf and held it up. "Congratulations! You're potty trained," he said. "Poop. That's what this card is talking about."

"That's a little different than telling someone to *eff*-off."

"I see your point. But the same amount of emotion, sometimes more is involved when you really want someone to fuck off as when you want to say *happy birthday* or *thank you.* What if your boss fired you? Wouldn't you want to send him a card that said *fuck off*?" Harley put the card back. "I would."

"Is this some kind of joke?"

People always assume it's a joke or the person is crazy when they address issues most people don't think about. "What if you had someone over to your house and they used your bathroom and really stunk up the place? Wouldn't you want to send them a card that said: *Thank you for making my house smell like shit?*"

"I suppose. But it would also be considered rude, not to mention immensely passive aggressive. If those types of cards interest you, then let me show you our humor section."

Harley followed her. The cards were not as crass as Harley had hoped, but some of them were amusing. The woman returned to her flower arrangement. There was a long silence before the woman picked up the shears again.

"I would like to say to you, young man, that it's more important in life to bring someone joy than humiliate them or point out their flaws. Cards and flowers are a gesture of kindness. Joy comes to those who give kindness."

"So you never get pissed at anyone?"

"Well, it never lasts very long. Besides, I work with flowers almost all day. What could ever keep me from enjoying a job like this? There's a saying. I think it's Buddha. It goes: *Holding on to anger is like grasping a hot coal with the intent of throwing it at someone else; you are the one who gets burned.*"

"Yeah, well Buddha didn't have gasoline."

The woman shook her head. "Is there anything else I can do for you?"

Harley carried a bouquet of lavender and white lilies through the parking lot to his car and drove to the toy store at the shopping mall across the street. Aisles of bright shiny rewards for children lay flush with the edges of the shelves. There were more toys than any child could possibly enjoy with what little time they had to be children. At Christmas time, parents would kill to strip the last toy from the shelf for the fuck-trophy who they hadn't gotten enough for already while other children asked for dads or moms or something other than tears for Christmas. The shelves were stacked with plastic figures—ultra buff army men and super voluptuous dolls dressed in pink—killing and fucking in the form of molded plastic two feet from the ground so children could learn their roles early.

At the back of the store, where they kept the cheaper, less extravagant toys, Harley found a fire truck for Joey. The peculiarity of searching for a gift struck him, and he glanced around looking for a sign of encouragement. He'd never bought anything for anyone, and all the gifts he had given were things he'd made for Maggie in grade school. Harley squatted and reached for a toy in the back, one that hadn't been vexed with the yearning brush of a child's fingers who couldn't have it.

Joey was at the kitchen table eating cereal and tracing his finger over a cartoon character printed on the back of the cereal box. Emily pushed her belly around the kitchen in her bathrobe. She waved at him through the window when he knocked.

"Hi, Joey," Harley said, entering the kitchen and handing Emily the flowers.

A tense look at the flowers, like he was handing her roadkill. "What are these for?"

"Nothing. I wanted to bring you joy."

He pulled the fire truck from behind his back and presented it to Joey. Joey's eyes bulged as he looked at it and stopped chewing. "This is for you."

Joey dropped his spoon and snatched the truck from Harley's hands. He was already in the living room smashing the new truck into the old before Emily could say anything.

"What the fuck are you doing?" she asked.

"What do you mean?"

"Why are you giving him things? You shouldn't be giving him things. Why are you giving me things?"

"I wanted to. I mean, I was just trying to be nice."

"You can be nice without bringing him gifts. I don't need your fucking handouts, or your goddamn flowers." She slapped the bouquet against his chest and moved to the stove. "I'm not your fucking charity case." She began stirring the pasta she had boiling.

"It's not like I'm giving you money or anything. I'm not trying to treat you like a charity case. I like you. I wanted to do something nice." Harley put the flowers on the table.

"Usually when people do something nice it's because they want something. With men it usually means they want one thing."

"It's not like that."

"Then what is it? Why are you trying to be so fucking nice to me?"

"I don't know."

Harley searched for some feeling. Some yearning for the words that would be the right thing to say. He faced off with Emily across the table. Glass fell and broke behind him, and Emily charged into the living room.

"What did you—"

And then there was the sound of a slap, and Harley turned to see the boy holding his face, tears about to explode out of him. The sound made the bones in his spine ache. Parts of his skin, where one of his mother's lovers used to strike, began to tingle. Joey began to wail. Harley walked into the living room where Joey was looking up at his mother, tears pouring from his eyes, his lips together and quivering. Pain was something reciprocal and Joey didn't deserve it. He hadn't hurt anyone. The tingling became a cold surrounding Harley's body.

"Why did you do that?"

Emily looked at him mouthing something, but she didn't make a sound. Joey scurried beneath the kitchen table, his back to the living room.

"Why did you do that?"

Emily shook her head. "I've never hit..."

"Then why now?"

"You don't know."

"I don't know what?"

"You have no idea what it's like. You don't understand."

"Neither does he."

"Do you know how hard it is to love someone who reminds you of someone you hate? Do you know what the fuck that's like? You come in here with flowers and toys and think that's going to make our life better?"

"Does causing him pain really make you feel better about

your own?"

Emily stepped to him, tilting her head and gritting her teeth at his chin.

"What? You want to know what my fucking life is like? What pain is like? Right now? Let me tell you about having a child at sixteen and another one on the way." She sucked tears from her top lip. "Your son, the thing that should be the most beautiful thing in the world...Here's the truth. You hate the eyes and nose and mouth and teeth and the body that develops below them because it reminds you of someone who hurt you, took your love and crushed it. Every day you wake this thing— this boy—to feed him, watch him eat at your kitchen table with you, and you wish the person you loved, the person you gave your heart to, the person who said everything was going to be alright...the person responsible for this could be there so you could be happy. But he's not. He's fucking not. He's gone. He chooses not to, so you hate *him* and everything about *him*. Even his child. But then you tell yourself, have to remind yourself sometimes that it's your child, so you have to love him. So, you love the good things, the things that remind you of you. That's what you love about the child, but there is always this thing you hate about him. And you choke this truth down every day because you're not supposed to feel that way at all. You're supposed to always love him. And you love him even more when you hurt him because his tears remind you so much of your own."

She took a step back and put her hands on her hips. Then she went to the kitchen and pulled Joey from beneath the table. Joey wrapped his arms around her, his tiny hand gripping the arm that had struck him. When Emily sat him on the couch, she held the sides of his face and pressed her lips into his forehead then she squeezed his face against her chest.

A faint whistle crept into his ears, the pitch of steam coming out of logs in a fire, and it took Harley a moment to realize that the sound came from his own breath against his lips. Emily turned her head toward him and pushed herself away from Joey. She gripped the sides of his face. A tight grip, and Harley waited for her to tell him to get out, to never talk to her again, but she didn't say anything. Instead, she pushed her lips against his. A dry tongue slid through the space in his teeth. Before he could react, she stopped.

"I'm sorry," she said. "Don't look for me at the school anymore. I'm not going back."

Harley knew it was coming—rejection, so he leaned his face toward hers, but she stopped him.

"I need to spend some time with Joey. But, if you want to see me, if you really want to see me, then I'll be here."

TWENTY-SIX

Bruno was smoking a cigarette at the back entrance of the gym when Harley moped into work on Monday. The bumper of her truck sagged under her weight where she leaned against it.

"You late."

"Yeah, Bruno. I'm sorry."

She pulled cigarettes from her shirt pocket. "Why you look sad? Have smoke."

"I don't really feel like one right now."

"Have smoke."

Harley took a cigarette and snapped open his Zippo. He took a pathetic puff that he couldn't handle. The second drag went deeper and filled his lungs with a tug that yanked fishhooks down his throat. He coughed out gray smoke that burned his nose and locked a gag between the roof of his mouth and the back of his tongue. Bruno chuckled.

Disgust as he looked at the cigarette, curious if the next drag would be different. It was. The third a little smoother, the pain duller. Harley finished the cigarette and stomped it out on the ground beside Bruno's.

"You tell Bruno why you look sad."

"I gave a girl flowers and she hated them."

"Why she hate flowers? They fake?"

"No. They were real. She said I shouldn't do nice things for her."

140

"She lie. All people like nice things. Stay nice."

"You think so?"

"Yes. I know this. Where is flower for Bruno?"

"I'll get you some tomorrow."

"I joke. Save money for girl."

The day started quiet as Harley descended into his janitorial duties. Most of the students, except the ones ditching class, were in the gymnasium for an assembly. Harley worked most of his thoughts over Joey and Emily, wondering if they were playing with the new fire truck, if Joey discovered what was wrong with his other one, and if he had forgotten how his mother had hurt him. He thought about how he made Emily laugh, and how different it was from everyone else's. People chuckled sometimes, when they overheard the things he said to people. Other times they whispered things about him and then laughed.

Halfway through the day, Ricky approached him from the other end of the hall. Sean trailed behind him, and for a moment, Harley wanted to leave the caddy and flee through exit at the end of the hallway. Before Ricky spoke, he kicked the trash barrel on the caddy onto the floor, spilling soiled paper towels and clear trash bags Harley had collected from classrooms.

"I thought I told you to stay away from Emily."

"I must have forgotten."

"Take it easy, Ricky. He might go home and cry to his mommy."

"I guess your night light will come in handy when she rocks me to sleep."

"I don't have a fucking nightlight."

"I'm not kidding, mop bitch. Stay the fuck away from Emily or next time I come back I'll be kicking more than your trash can."

"Oh, please, Ricky. Don't do that. I don't think I could handle my trash can being in danger any longer. Please, Ricky, please don't hurt my trash—"

Ricky slammed a fist into his gut and doubled him over. His

diaphragm rippled beneath his lungs, keeping him from breathing.

"I mean it, mop bitch."

Air rushed into Harley as the two boys walked away. He pressed his cheek against the side of the trash can. Tears slid down his face and rolled over the rubbery material to the tile floor.

One of Maggie's boyfriends used to jab Harley in the stomach with his fingers. He worked construction for the highway department and spent the winter months, while he was laid off, watching court TV and drinking low-price beer Maggie brought home for him from work. She would leave Harley with him when she had weekend shifts. Harley would often attempt to interact with the man but in doing so would stand in front of the television. The man would extend his fingers and jab the tips of them into Harley's stomach without the use of words or an expression of anger. Harley would reel back and giggle until the man did it hard enough for Harley to know it wasn't a game. When the pain came, he merely watched the man with misunderstanding from a few feet. The nightly pain in his stomach and his crying would wake his mother, frustrated, until the blood in his stool convinced her to bring him to the hospital.

Harley got to his feet and reorganized his caddy. He pushed the caddy past Mr. Reed's door to the end of the hall to empty the trash cans there. Most of the time, the only trash in them were hall passes students threw out as they were ditching school. Both the cans were empty. Harley cleaned the glass on the heavy steel doors and picked up a pen cap and a lunch straw from the corner behind the trash can. Mr. Reed was in the hallway a few feet behind him when Harley turned.

"Sorry if I missed your trash pickup, Mr. Reed. I'm still trying to remember everything."

He shook his head. "Not about that. I was wondering if I could talk to you for a minute."

"Sure."

He walked back to his classroom and Harley followed, leaving the caddy behind. Harley hadn't spoken to him since he was sent to the boys' home. Reed shut the door behind them.

"What the hell are you doing?" Reed asked, sitting at his desk.

"What do you mean?"

"I mean, why the hell are you cleaning up trash and shitters in your old high school?" He kicked his feet up on the corner of an open drawer.

"Jobs are hard to find, and I'm trying to save enough money to move out of my mother's."

"Now you're working as a janitor in the high school you attended."

"Yeah. It seems promising."

"You always were such a smart ass. What happened with Emily Jensen?"

"What do you mean?"

Reed pulled a pencil from his desk and began tapping the eraser against his thumbnail. "There's a rumor you brought her home the other day."

"I gave her a ride home. Are you concerned for her safety or something?"

"Actually, I'm concerned about yours. Ricky's not dumb enough to do something in school. His father would kill him if his athletic career was jeopardized, but off school property, well, that's different."

"Ricky is too dumb to be in school. What else would his parents worry about, besides athletics?"

"It never ends." Mr. Reed shook his head and chuckled. "How's your mother doing?"

"I figured it wouldn't take long before you asked about her."

"She was always a big concern for you. She still drinking?"

"No, but now I wish she would."

"Oh, why's that?"

"I was kidding. She's just difficult to live with, that's all."

"Are you looking for a place now?"

"Not right now, but hopefully soon."

"I have a loft, and..." Reed trailed off.

Harley thought he might have been changing his mind.

"It's forward of me but you're welcome to it. It's above the garage, if you need a place to stay until you find something better."

"How much do you want for that?"

"I don't want any money. I'll need some help around the house on the weekends. We'll consider that payment. You can save some money for an apartment and think about going to school."

"Why are you being so nice to me?"

"Nothing wrong with being nice to people, is there?"

"Can I look at the place after work?"

"Sure."

Reed lived at the end of a cul-de-sac in a blue Cape with a one car garage on the other side of the driveway. There were flower beds around the house but nothing had been planted that year. The lawn was patched with dying grass left from a bird bath, a tarp, a two-by-four, and a rolled-up, water-swollen newspaper that were all in a pile in front of the garage door. There was a stack of lumber beside the garage, pressure treated. A shadow moved behind the picture window and Reed came out.

They walked into the backyard where he showed Harley how he wanted to build a deck on the back of the house. There was brush growing through rusted hunks of metal that had to be removed. The roof needed to be shingled and the house needed paint. Reed led him up the steps through the back entrance of the garage. The loft was sweltering. Harley began sweating after a few minutes. Reed assured him that it wasn't as humid with the garage door open. He found the light switch and brought more heat into the room.

"It's pretty hot in here, I know, but with a couple of fans it's not so bad."

"That which doesn't kill us makes us stronger," Harley said and wandered away from Reed to the far side of loft.

"You a fan of Nietzsche?"

Harley looked over the rafters above him. "No. Conan."

There was a circulation fan above the door. Reed turned that on as well. An easel leaned into the rafters and a futon sat against the wall opposite the door. There wasn't much to the room except that it would be a space for Harley that he wouldn't have to share with Sean and Maggie. Reed had leaned over and was going through a box of books. He noticed Harley watching him.

"My wife left these," he said, fanning the pages of a novel in his fingers.

"Where did she go?"

"Back to Poughkeepsie to stay with her mother. Twelve years we were married. Seems like it was only days."

"Why'd she leave?"

"Well, we didn't agree on most things. I wanted kids. She didn't. Didn't make much sense for her to stay. That kind of disagreement isn't usually resolved."

"I thought all women wanted kids. That's weird."

"She didn't think it was fair that women bear most of the burden. I didn't think it was fair for me to ask her to, so we split. No hard feelings really. I helped her pack, paid for the movers, and waved her goodbye."

"Do you still talk to her?"

"Nah. Better that way."

"Probably."

Reed gave Harley a confused look then shook it off as he stood. "Well, I'm going to let you get acquainted with the place. I'll get you a key."

Reed went out, and Harley's body grew acclimated to the room's temperature. He looked around and thought of how he would arrange furniture in the place if he'd had any. The move would be easy. He had nothing at Maggie's except some clothes and random objects of Sean's that Harley was already commit-ted to stealing. The futon was comfortable and he sat on it wondering why Reed's wife didn't want children. He seemed like a decent man. It didn't seem fair that so many children were born to parents who would screw up their lives before they had a chance to screw it up on their own. He wondered if Maggie was going to do that, or Emily. Harley thought about Emily more and became excited over the thought of having her at his new place. Harley thought about her until he convinced himself that he needed to see her.

Harley took the opportunity to gather the things he wanted at Maggie's while she and Sean weren't there. He filled a small box with items from the house—an alarm clock, the toaster, the television remote, a couch cushion, a fly swatter, a roll of tin-foil, an ashtray, all the forks, all the toilet paper including the one on the roller. The box was full, and moving out of Maggie's gave him a sense of accomplishment. He threw the box and his duffel bag of clothes in the back seat and went back for the snow globe. As he sat on his bed with the snow globe in his hands, he imagined what kind of family or couple would live in a place like that, whether they were perpetually content or if they were trapped in a continual state of torment, blaming their tribulations on the shaky hand of God.

Before Harley left the driveway, he took another look at the house. It seemed strange and frightening that he wouldn't be going through that door anymore. Liberating that he wouldn't have to face Sean and Maggie anymore.

TWENTY-SEVEN

Harley waited outside of Emily's on the hood of his car while she changed out of her house clothes. A lime green Mustang slowed at the intersection down the street. A moment later, the tires squealed, and the car sped off. Emily came out of the house wearing a yellow dress. The dress stopped at her knee and the small curving muscles of her quadriceps flexed in the shape of inverted hearts as she walked toward him. Harley opened the passenger door and she crab-walked over the seat.

She fanned her fingers over the backrest, pointing to the boxes. "What's with all the stuff?"

"I'm moving out of my mother's."

"Well look at you making strides toward independence. Setting up a bachelor pad?"

"If you consider a bag of clothes and a futon a bachelor pad."

"Sounds exactly like a bachelor pad."

"Good, then you can be my first victim."

"That's not creepy at all."

"I can step it up a notch, if that's what turns you on."

"Ew, don't."

The silence between them made him think of the times he'd annoyed Maggie or one of her lovers, and the subsequent time he spent shunned and ignored, when he would climb under his bed to the far corner against the wall and sleep with his arm wrapped around the snow globe.

"Tell me about your new place," Emily asked.

"Reed's letting me stay in the loft above his garage."

"Well that's cool. Are you going to show me?"

Harley pulled away from the curb and the Mustang crossed the intersection again. He made the short drive to his new place. Emily pushed out of the seat holding her stomach. Her hips swayed as she climbed the steps ahead of him to the loft. Behind her, he couldn't tell she was pregnant. Sunlight spilled through the gaps of her legs and into his eyes as she made each step. Harley thought about how safe it was beneath her dress—how her baby enjoyed the feeling of warmth, how the loft would finally be his shelter from the world he was leaving behind at Maggie's.

They entered the loft and Harley hit the switch for the circulation fan. It whined at first then circled, swooping dust from the collar ties and forcing them to dance in the band of light coming through the door. The air smelled of pine and cedar. Emily sat on the futon and looked up into the rafters. Hair stuck to her temples where she had begun to sweat.

"Nice place."

"Thanks."

"It's hot, though."

"I'll put some fans in here."

"And there are no windows."

Harley felt embarrassed by her observations. She was right and the whole space seemed like some dark, humid cave where he would try to sleep but probably not be able to because of how hot it would get. Harley saw himself thrashing around on the futon at night attempting to rest, the fabric and his skin slick from perspiration. He began to feel unsafe, that he should return to Maggie's.

"You're going to need some things for your place," Emily said. "There's a big yard sale down in the parking lot of the bowling alley."

"Who has a yard sale on a Monday? Who goes to a yard sale

on a Monday?"

"Housewives and old people."

"Do you want to go?" he asked.

"Sure."

She took the stairs one at a time on the way down holding the railing and her stomach with caution. In the car, she sang with whatever song was playing on the radio and because her voice was something joyful, Harley let the songs play even though he hated them. She dropped a hand from her stomach and reached over for his hand. Harley drew it away and she scowled at him.

"What's your problem? Is there something wrong with holding my hand?"

"No. I just don't like it."

"You don't like it or you don't want to?"

"I don't see why people hold hands."

"It's a form of affection."

"So are hand jobs."

"That'll go over well in public."

"We're in my car right now."

"You're not getting a hand job. Besides, that is totally different than holding hands."

"How?"

"Because it's explicitly sexual. Holding hands is not."

"What if my hand is on my dick?"

"You're ridiculous," she huffed and stared out the window.

"How am I ridiculous? Holding hands is ridiculous. It looks stupid."

"It's what people do."

"Exactly. And people look stupid at just about everything they do. If we want to look stupid, we should just hold onto each other's ear lobes and walk around wishing everyone we see a happy birthday."

She laughed. Then her expression quickly went straight and hard and almost shocked like something had jumped out of her ear and bit her face. "You're a jackass."

"Thank you."

She shook her head and Harley pulled into the parking lot at the bowling alley. The people walking around looked the same as the people selling their piles of junk. There were men wearing denim shorts, knee-high socks, and fanny packs to hold their money in, men who obviously bought most of their clothing at surplus stores and yard sales. Emily and Harley perused boxes of fractured knickknacks and clocks, stacks of old books that smelled like hay barns, and clothes outdated by three decades. There were children's toys and rusty tools. There was nothing at the rummage festival Harley wanted, not even enough to steal. More people came and women haggled down sellers by the nickel. Harley listened to one man say he could pay only five dollars for an aluminum step ladder because he didn't want to break a hundred. The seller gave in and cut his price in half. The man carried the ladder to his car then went into the store next to the parking lot and came out with a cup of coffee. Emily said there were more yard sales in town and suggested they drive around looking.

They took every side street marked by a cardboard sign stapled to a telephone pole. Harley sifted through the items people no longer wanted, or things that belonged to dead relatives they'd finally gotten the courage to take from the attic and get rid of. At the end of the rummage pursuit, Harley had purchased a small oak coffee table and a framed picture of Audrey Hepburn because Emily resembled her so much. She blushed when he told her so. In all, he spent seven dollars and fifty cents. It was a breezy afternoon and Harley enjoyed in the smell of Emily wafting in as they passed each other during their search of secondhand treasures.

Harley led the way up to the loft with the coffee table when they returned to his place. He found a nail to suspend the picture he'd bought and spent a few frustrating minutes trying to get the frame to balance until Emily urged him over to her.

Her eyes focused on his chest and the corners of her mouth twitched. She grabbed for his hands and tilted her head up. Tiny fingers pressed the blood vessels in his wrists. Harley's pulse surged into the parts of her fingers where the prints coiled down to nothing. She still had her tongue on her lips when he bent to kiss her and she bit at him. The kissing became faster. She knew what she was doing. Harley didn't know how to breathe while he kissed her, so he didn't. Her hands up along the inside of his legs to his belt and she took his penis out. Harley exhaled hard in one loud sigh into her mouth, feeling the compression ease from the throbbing. Her clammy palms made her movement dry and the friction was painful, but painful in the way that a child yanks a tooth from his mouth for the tooth fairy—square bloody teeth showing in a smile with the thought of reward.

Emily pulled her lips from his and tilted her head. A warm gulp of air surrounded the tip of his dick. It continued down and he could feel the slick rigidness of her palate, the warm pressure of her tongue, and the sharpness of her teeth pressuring the thick vein running down his shaft. She grabbed his wrists again and pulled his hands to her breasts. Emily pulled him out of her mouth then shoved him back in, a little deeper that time pushing his pants to his ankles. He squeezed his eyes shut and tried to picture her face, Emily's, but he couldn't. Her tongue worked side to side with him in her mouth and his head fell back, too heavy for his neck to hold up. His vision went white and his legs tensed until his knees felt as though they were going to snap backwards. Her lip touched the bottom of his stomach and Maggie's face came into his vision. He came hard, like a million tiny fists were surging out of him and trying to punch a hole in the back of her throat. He saw nothing but white and Emily's teeth scraped along his flesh. She choked, sucked at the air, and pushed hard against his hips. She raged into a gurgling cough and his pants stopped his attempt to step backwards and he fell. Something hard slammed against the back of his head and a ringing burst into his ears. Everything around him went black.

TWENTY-EIGHT

Maggie came in the house after her shift with a quart of vanilla ice cream that had partially melted on the ride home. She rolled her eyes at the missing couch cushion and sat on the floor. Several minutes into an episode of *Passions*, she saw through Harley's open bedroom door that his snow globe was not on the windowsill where he kept it. It always waited for him on the sill, untouched, and the swirling specks that she would sometimes see settling to the bottom of it were always an indication that he was home. She bought it for him on his fifth Christmas, but over the years had forgotten where she bought it and wondered why it was the only object he'd ever attached himself to.

She left the ice cream container on the floor beside the couch and wandered into his room. His drawers were empty. She traced her fingers along the edge of the dresser and took a seat on his bed. The sheets were worn down to threads, and the coils in the mattress were contracted and flat. It was the most uncomfortable piece of furniture she had ever touched. Maggie thought of the nights she found him sleeping on the couch or in the back seat of her car before he had been sent to the boys' home. The growl in her stomach reminded her of how she'd felt being pregnant with him, and how she felt then, at that moment. She left Harley's room and turned off the television wishing she knew what to make of the feelings she had, a stomach full of air, and a house quiet with an unfamiliar silence.

Maggie sat on the floor where she'd been before inspecting Harley's room. After a few minutes she got up to shut the door. An eerie desperation gnawed at her. She wondered if Harley'd just taken his things, if he would surprise her in the morning with his appearance at the table or if he'd actually moved out. Briefly, she wondered what the following days would allow her—relief from the dread of his presence? She asked herself this but didn't feel it. The dread of his absence, his leaving, bordered on abandonment. She grew angry. What right did he have to leave her?

TWENTY-NINE

Harley awoke to the sound of Emily's voice and the gentle tapping of her fingers against his cheek. He thought he'd been out for hours because the room was completely black as if the lights had been turned off. The back of his head felt crushed and he strained in the darkness to see her, his back itchy from the grit on the floor of the loft.

"Are you okay?" she asked. Her voice came at him loud and heavy, unexpected. Darkness demanded whispers and quiet. Everything was so loud around him.

"My head. Turn the lights on," he said trying to focus.

"I did."

"Then why can't I see?"

There was nothing but tiny white specks dancing in the darkness.

"This isn't funny," she said.

He moved his head from side to side.

"I know it's not funny. Turn the fucking lights on."

"The goddamn lights are on! They're on! They're on! Please stop doing this."

"I can't see."

Harley bent his knees and worked his pants up to his waist and got to his feet. Panic and chaos bounced through his mind as he scrambled around the room reaching out for the walls, searching for some stability—some safety. He tripped over the coffee table and fell to the floor again. The floor brought a taste of cardboard and leather as his lips pressed against it. He froze. The darkness was petrifying.

Like the slow seep of water through a crevice, Harley's vision began to come back, but it returned with a searing needles of light that forced him to close his eyes. He tried to open them again but the shape of the objects around him cut through his vision like broken bits of glass. Emily's voice swirled around him. Again he tried to open his eyes to see her but the light made his eyes feel as though they were being squeezed tightly in the hands of a cruel child.

Emily helped him to the car. Harley became aware of the loudness of his own breathing and hers. The things he touched, the pavement under his feet, glass, dashboard, door handle, all brought a fearful curiosity. The Maverick sputtered to life, and he reached for something to hold. His fingers worked across the upholstery of the seat until he found her hand and latched on, the sensation of drowning spilling over him. He held her hand to the hospital, through the doctor's questions, until the doctor put him onto a slab that slowly moved him into a tube that felt much like a coffin with slightly more elbow room.

It was cold in the machine and it moved only a few inches at a time. Then, it rattled somewhere inside drowning out the beeps and compressions of its other functions. He tried to sleep, to dream, to see something other than the pale light behind his eye-lids, even just a glimmer of something comforting. After the test they put him in a wheelchair and a nurse pushed him through doors that sighed and clicked when they opened. Harley waited for a long time in a small quiet room with Emily for the doctor to come.

The doctor's approach was quiet, and there was only the click of the door handle to warn Harley of his presence. Sheets of paper flipped in front of him. A pen clicked, and then the doctor's voice.

"Mr. Remick," he said.

"Yeah?"

"We've gone over the results of your CT scan. You have a concussion and there is a contusion on the occipital lobe, which is why your vision is impaired."

Harley tapped his eyelids with the tips of his middle fingers. "So what does that mean? I have brain damage?"

"Not in the way that you might be referring. Your vision should be normal within a few hours. You'll probably have some headaches though as your pupils begin to readjust."

"So my vision will return to normal?"

"Yes. I do want you to be supervised for the next couple of days because of the concussion. You'll need to be woken up every couple of hours to ensure there is no memory loss or other issues."

"Brain damage," he shouted. Harley slapped his palms against the top of his head. "You said I didn't have brain damage. Does this mean I'm retarded?"

"Ms. Jensen, will you be staying with Harley?"

"Yes."

"Be sure to wake him up frequently if he does sleep. Ask him questions. *What's your name? Where are you?* Those types of things. If his answers are incorrect or inconsistent, call us right away."

"How am I supposed to know my location when I can't open my eyes? Emily, are you sure this is a doctor?"

The doctor clicked his pen again.

When they got out to the car, Emily helped him into the seat. "Everything's going to be alright."

Harley waited for the sounds of her climbing into the driver's seat. Keys jingled, and a moment later, a click. Then another.

"There's something wrong," she said.

"Do you want me to get out and see what the problem is?"

"Are you being a dick?"

"No."

Another series of clicks.

"The car won't start. What do we do?" she asked.

"Guess you're going to have to guide me home."

"Yeah but it's dark out."

"I can see that."

She giggled and got out of the car. Harley pushed his door open and attempted to step out. The seat belt jerked him back into place and gave him a small friction burn on his neck. Emily laughed a little louder. The seat belt sucked across his chest when he unhooked it and he reached for the sides of the door to guide himself out of the car. Harley stood and smashed the top of his head into the edge of the roof and flopped back down in the seat once more. Pain screamed across the top of his skull and burned down the sides of his face. Emily didn't laugh like he expected her to, like everyone else would have. She pressed her hands against the sides of his face.

"Just stop moving before you hurt yourself worse."

Harley rubbed the pain from the top of his head. Emily took his hand and they started home. Breaks in the sidewalk attempted to trip him. Cars rolled by, and he moved closer to her each time one passed. The sound of cars seemed to come down the sidewalk right toward them. His hands trembled. Emily warned him to step down from the sidewalk when they crossed streets.

"I'm sorry for ruining your day," Harley said after they'd crossed the street and were only a short distance from the loft.

"You didn't ruin my day."

Heat had built itself in the loft and it fell on Harley like a long, annoying hug. Emily got him to the futon and pulled his shoes from his feet. He fell asleep despite the heat, and Emily woke him after what seemed like only a few minutes. His mouth felt sticky and decayed.

"What's your name?" She asked him.

"Keyser Söze."

"Not funny. What's your name?"

"Paul Keller."

"I mean it. What's your name?"

"Don't you find it a little funny that you're asking the man you're in bed with what his name is?"

"I don't find that funny at all. Now, what's your name?"

"Harley Remick."

THIRTY

The next morning Harley woke with his hands moving over the curves of Emily's body and he thought of a mountainous landscape in his hands breaking through the trees in the distance on some state route that led to nowhere. Emily's deep breaths made the landscape rise. The loft came into focus and a headache settled against the inside of his skull behind his ears. He closed his eyes. The heat of Emily's stomach and the baby moving inside her forced him to pull his hands from beneath her T-shirt and roll to his back.

With his eyes closed, gravity became an entirely new demon. Even on the futon, on the second floor of the garage, felt like he was sinking into the earth and folds of dirt were rising over the edges of his body petrifying him from moving out of fear he would only sink deeper. His hearing became more acute, regardless of how much noise he tried to ignore. Dust whistled through the air and the wood moaned, whispering back to the heat pressing against it.

Footsteps hit the stairs outside and the lean of them and the creak of the nails revealed which step was being pressed by what foot and how hard the person was pulling on the railing on his way up to the loft door. The slap of the soles of a pair of sandals stopped suddenly outside the door and the doorknob shook. Emily exhaled a hot, rotten breath against his face and the door shuddered opened.

"Hey—" Reed froze, peering in at Harley and Emily on the futon.

Emily pushed herself up on the bed. Harley waited for one of them to speak.

Reed spoke first. "What's going on?" There was a terse urgency in his voice. Harley knew that tone, from class, before he sent someone out of the room. Harley kept his eyes closed intent on milking his injury until Reed left.

"Nothing," Emily said, and the sense of guilt and shame was obvious in her voice.

"I fell," Harley said to the air above his face.

"What?"

"It was an accident," Emily said.

"I don't think you can describe something like this as an accident."

"I can't open my eyes."

"What?"

"Last night," Emily cleared her throat. "He fell against the coffee table." Her weight shifted on the bed. "We had to go to the emergency room. The doctor said he had a concussion."

"I can't open my eyes and I have brain damage."

"A concussion?"

"And I can't open my eyes."

Footsteps approached the futon and Emily's weight shifted again. Cool air fanned against the corners of his eyes. Snapping fingers. Harley twitched away from the snapping.

"What did the doctor say?"

"He should be woken up often and asked his name and location."

"I might be retarded."

"Is there anything he has to do?"

"I have to be watched very carefully."

"Emily, I can take you home if you'd like. Harley, I'll call out today."

"No. I want her to stay here," Harley blurted.

Reed's voice caught. "Well. I—I think it would be better if I looked after you."

Harley clutched Emily's hand. Her breathing was quicker and through her nose.

"I want her here."

"Emily is in no condition to be caring for you."

"I'm in no condition to be without her."

"I think that should be left up to Emily."

"It's okay. Really, Mr. Reed. I don't mind looking after him."

"Suit yourself. Let me know if you need anything."

"I will," Harley said.

"Yeah, I meant Emily, Harley."

Reed slipped out of the room. Emily's belly pressed against Harley's arm. She loosed her fingertips against Harley's skin and let them run wild over the ticklish crevices between his ribs.

"That was awkward." She yawned. "I'm tired. Do you care if I go back to sleep?"

He rocked his head. Her breaths fell deep and slow and soon she was asleep. Behind his eyelids, Harley saw colorful, looping images come to his mind.

The neighbor cranked his lawnmower and pushed the loud, sputtering machine out across his lawn to butcher grass. The lawn had been mowed just a couple days before. Pain rushed along the sides of Harley's head when he opened his eyes. The lawnmower paced the lawn.

"Are you hungry?" Emily asked. Her voice came hard into his ear and he jerked away. "Oh, I'm sorry. I didn't mean to scare you." She held the side of his face and kissed his ear.

"A little, I guess."

"Do you want to walk down to Jay's Grille? It's not far from here."

"Sure."

She pushed herself to the edge of the bed and her weight left the futon. "Did you want to change your clothes?"

"No. I'll go in this."

"What should we do about your car?"

"You can have it."

"Gee, thanks."

"You're welcome. What time is it?"

"Early."

She held the backs of his hands and guided Harley to the door, allowing him to feel the knob. Outside the door, she put his hand on the railing and wrapped an arm around him until they reached the bottom of the stairs. The lawnmower growled close to them, then faded.

Emily led Harley over the cracked sidewalk, around trash cans, and over tree roots until the air was filled with the smell of grease and exhaust from cars awaiting their to-go orders. Inside the restaurant, voices cluttered the air along with metallic sounds in the kitchen. They sat on a cool smooth bench that reminded Harley of the seats attached to the desks in school. The lighting in the place was dim and Harley squinted over the menu fighting to ignore his headache.

After they ordered, the sounds and smells began to bother Harley. The server rushed by their table. Cooks yelled line orders and notified the server when they were ready. Forks and knives dug into ceramic. The sweat and heft of the person sitting on the bench behind Harley became noticeable as the person leaned back and forth over their food. It was after Harley and Emily received their food that Harley grew attentive to the loud smacking of the person behind. He tried to ignore it, but couldn't, and his irritation grew until the sound was torturing.

"Who is eating behind me?" he asked Emily.

"I don't know."

"They sound like a cow."

"Shhhh. You're speaking too loud."

The smacking stopped. Harley smelled cat piss and sweat—the odor of a person who ate nothing but fried food—a person who used their clothes as a napkin and had a large mouth that they never introduced a toothbrush to. Someone who gorged themselves and who could chew loud enough to drown out the growling stomachs of starving children.

"I don't care if I'm speaking too loud. I can barely hear myself speak without hearing that person chew. It's annoying, and it sounds worse than someone shitting diarrhea."

Heft shifted from the bench, and the clumping of feet pivoted toward Harley's table. "You got a problem?" the man asked.

"No. I chew with my mouth closed. See?" Harley guided his burger slowly into his mouth and took a bite. He turned his face toward the obese man and chewed dramatically, but with his mouth closed.

"Maybe you should keep eating so your mouth stays shut."

"He has a concussion," Emily said.

"He doesn't need to be looking for another one."

"You don't need to eat like livestock. Shut your jowls when you chew."

The man slapped his palms on the table and ducked into Harley's face. "I told you to shut your mouth."

"And if you shut yours, we wouldn't be having this conversation, lard-ass."

"Alright," the waitress interrupted. "The two of you need to leave."

"We're not together." Harley waved a finger between himself and the fat man.

The waitress pointed at Harley and Emily. "I'm speaking to you two."

"I'm not paying if you're kicking us out."

"The bill is $14.93. You can pay and leave, or I can call the cops."

"Great. More pigs."

"Harley, let's leave, please."

Harley pulled a ten and a five from his pocket and dropped it onto the pile of ketchup on his plate. "Keep the change," he said as they stood from their booth. At the door, Harley spoke again.

"Carcass swallowing lard-ass pig fucking rot smelling blob of shit mouth-breathing motherfucker." He began laughing.

The fat man rocked to get out of his booth.

"Come on," Emily said and jerked his arm to pull him from the door.

They strode through the parking lot, quickening their steps as the fat man yelled to them from the door of the restaurant. Harley was still laughing.

"This isn't funny. Why are you laughing?"

"I fucking hate fat people."

"You hate fat people?"

"Yes."

They slowed to a walk as they moved uphill.

"We can cut through the school playground back to your place," Emily said.

Branches of trees hanging over the sidewalk shaded them from the sun during parts of their walk and Harley could open his eyes a little wider. As they moved from shadow to sunlight, strokes of heat burned against his neck and cheeks. Emily took a brisk pace, dragging him high stepping behind her.

When they reached to top of the stairs to the loft, Emily was panting. They entered the space and the smell of grass and trees and summer air disappeared, replaced with the stagnant wood smell of the loft.

"I need to lie down," Emily said, moving to the futon.

He lay beside her. Images from the past day rolled through Harley's head and he thought about her mouth. He reached for her hand, but she pushed it away. Then he remembered whose face he'd seen just before he'd come in Emily's mouth.

THIRTY-ONE

Sean rolled off Maggie and apologized. It had been quick, and Maggie had only had time to slide her hand down his back before he came. Just a few minutes before that, she'd told him she was pregnant. Sean's reaction was to reach for her pants. Now, he was sliding his back on. She didn't tell him that coming prematurely was alright like she had done the past couple of times.

"Do you have somewhere to be?" she asked, regretting her question.

"I'm meeting some friends."

"Oh. Well, do you want some dinner waiting when you get home?"

"Yeah, that'd be great."

Maggie climbed from the bed. She pulled her robe from the floor and swung it through the air as she fed her arms through the sleeves.

"What would you like?"

"Whatever. Doesn't matter."

"Oh, good. I'll surprise you. Leave your laundry, too. I'll make sure that's done as well."

Sean tied his sneakers. "Awesome."

"Maybe I can go do some shopping. Anything you want me to get?"

"No. Not really. Beer maybe."

"Sure thing." Maggie left the room as Sean rummaged through

the drawers for a clean shirt.

Sean came from the bedroom to face Maggie leaned against the back of a chair. "What?" he asked.

"Could you do me a favor on your way home?"

"What?"

"Die in a car accident."

"Why would you say that?"

"It would be a lot easier for me to throw your things out if you were dead."

"What's your problem?"

"My problem? Are you fucking kidding me? You can't fuck me to save your life, and you run out the minute—second, I should say—that you're finished and you don't think there's anything wrong with that, and I have a problem? How about you grow the fuck up and start to take some responsibility around here."

"What do you want me to do? I'm busy with school and other things. Why are you bitching at me just because you got pregnant?"

Maggie's cheeks flared hot and she clenched her teeth. "*I* got pregnant? *We* got pregnant, Sean. It's our baby."

"Well how am I supposed to know it's mine?"

She sucked a sharp breath through her nose. "Where the fuck do you get the balls to say that to me?"

"Where? Right here in my pants, bitch." Sean waved a hand through the air and grabbed his crotch.

Maggie had never thrown a punch and when she connected against the end of Sean's nose, her wrist bent and a sharp pain pulsed up her forearm. Sean staggered back and held his hands under his chin to catch the blood running from his nose as if somehow he could put it back. He bumped into the refrigerator on his way to the stove for the rag hanging from the handle of the oven. Maggie, slightly bent over and holding her wrist, watched him, more concerned about the pain in her arm than what Sean was going to do. She waited for him to turn toward her, holding the rag against his nose and tilting his head back slightly. Recently, at work, Maggie learned that people shouldn't tilt their head back when they have a nosebleed. She kept it to herself.

"I think you broke my nose."

"It's not that great of a nose, Sean. You'll be alright. Get the fuck out. Don't come back."

Maggie straightened and repositioned her wrist against her waist. She moved into the living room and slumped against the couch.

"Are you serious?" Sean asked from the doorway.

Maggie continued her stare and nodded.

"You know, none of this shit would have happened if you hadn't let your loser fucking kid back here. This is fucking bullshit. I didn't do anything to deserve this, you fucking whore. That's what it is, isn't it? You find someone else to screw. I remember how I met you. I should have known you were a fucking dumpster cunt. Fucking slut."

Sean charged into the room and gripped the back of the couch on either side of Maggie's head. "You sneaky fucking slut. That's exactly it, isn't it? You tried to blame me for you spreading your legs and getting knocked up by someone else. You know who the father of this kid's going to be or is it going to be just like that other fucking waste of air?"

Maggie raised her chin to look into Sean's eyes. All that Harley had said to her rung true. It was *her* kid. "It's not your kid," she told him.

Sean smirked. "That's what I thought." He pushed himself from Maggie's face and swatted her cheek with his fingertips. "Fucking skank."

Sean walked toward the bedroom. Maggie kept her face against the couch cushion, where it stopped moving after Sean slapped her. Her hair tickled her neck where it was disheveled and she left it there feeling the sting on her face and the pain in her wrist. Sean flung his clothes into bags in her room—the reclaimed section of home that she no longer had to share—a vacancy that she could fill with another the same way she had in the past. She thought of her past lovers and their words echoing in silent rooms, their empty promises. She'd grasped for a fragment of youth, clung to the shards of broken dreams willing to hang on and bleed, but Sean hadn't said much that she hadn't heard before. Even his footsteps sounded the same. The packing of his things, too, that violent fabric shoving into bags and boxes. The emphasized breathing, the last footsteps to the door, the door slamming, and the ringing in her ears from the rush of air through the apartment.

THIRTY-TWO

Harley's hopes of his headache going away were futile. It didn't leave when Emily had to go back to Joey or when Reed checked on him before heading into school. Harley squinted at blurry lumps of things around him. In that time, he measured the distance to the walls from the futon and the door. He discovered there were fourteen steps to the loft and on steps seven and ten, going up, there were splinters in the railing. The yard was thirty paces from the bottom steps of the loft to the wooden fence. He lay in the grass most days, and let it pass over his face until he'd learned to tell the time by how warm the sun felt against his skin.

The pain did diminish after a few days, and one afternoon while Harley was sprawled out on the dying grass of the lawn, Reed sat next to him.

"How's the vision today?"

"The vision is fine, now, but I still have a bit of a headache."

"Harley, I think we should talk."

Harley sat up in the grass and supported his weight with his elbows. "About what?"

"Your relationship with Emily."

"What about it?"

Reed pulled a tuft of grass from the lawn. "I don't think you should be seeing her."

Harley's insides rattled. His elbows went limp and he jerked back. "Why not?"

"Do you really care for her? Why would you want to subject yourself to someone with so much baggage?"

"We all have baggage, don't we?"

"Yeah. I guess that's true, but there is so much more available to you, Harley." Reed's breathing grew louder and Harley could feel his exhales against his neck. "Are you sure she's what you want?" he whispered, placing a hand on Harley's shoulder and rubbing his thumb in a circular motion.

Harley leaned away. "I don't know what I want."

Reed tapped Harley's back and went into his house. Harley felt the unease of what had just happened though he wasn't exactly sure why he felt uneasy. Reed's words, however, spun him into more confusion. There hadn't been a man to tell Harley what was right or what choices he should consider—that perpetual ache of not knowing the mystery of where he'd come from, who his father was. His only knowledge of making the right choices came from watching his mother make the wrong ones. Men were supposed to care about women, but sometimes they cared only about what they could get from them. Harley forgot about Reed and focused on Emily. He liked having her around. He'd never had someone like her to talk to or anyone for that matter.

He spent a day pacing beneath the rafters of the loft. His headache was dulling it seemed, but Harley wondered if he was only getting used to the pain. He took long periods of time concentrating on a path before him thinking of Maggie and Emily and imagined what they wanted from him. They wanted men, he knew that, but what kind? Thoughts of a father gave him a reason to think about the term and what types of men define it. Sometimes, fathers are companions to their sons. They teach them about baseball, how to bait a fishing hook, and how to throw a punch. There are the fathers who force their children into every activity imaginable, ballet, piano lessons, football, and more. They force their children into a life *they* believe will be better. There are the drunk bastards who, in their brief and limited moments of sobriety, got their high-school sweetheart pregnant in the back seat of their father's Chevy, or under the stadium bleachers, who use their kids to stomp the dust off their boots. There are fathers who steal the seed of their daughters before it could even sprout—before it could ever have a chance to blossom. There are all kinds of fathers, but the only thing Harley knew about a father was that it was the label used to define an appendage that wasn't there—an amputated thumb.

Reed came into the loft as Harley sat on the futon—a daily ritual at that point, Reed checking in on him.

"How are you feeling?" he asked.

"I don't know."

"Is something wrong?"

"No. There's nothing wrong."

"Okay. I'll be out for a while. There's food in the fridge if you're hungry. The door's locked, but the lock box code for the spare key is 7-9-3-2-8."

What Harley thought about, after Reed, was Maggie, her face in his mind during his first sexual encounter with a woman. Maggie was repulsed by him, and any act of kindness she'd ever displayed was no more than a fetching gesture to recall the past and her neglect. She had no love for him. Love is what you want but can't have. It's the invisible, corrupt agenda that drains the faith of its believers.

When the automatic sprinkler began flitting in the yard next door, Harley left the loft and went into Reed's house. The drapes over the picture window in the living room diluted the light coming in. It was darkness much like the gloom in the garage. By the kitchen sink there was an ashtray. Half a menthol cigarette was crushed and broken at the filter. Inside the refrigerator were samples of things from the health food aisle at the grocery store. Everything was organic—yogurt, cottage cheese, hydrogen-free peanut butter, tofu, soy milk, all expensive and tasteless. There was no meat, and when Harley closed the refrigerator door he saw a PETA pamphlet on the freezer. Harley lifted the bottom corner of the pamphlet and shook his head. Another organization maddened by their belief in what was right. They use plastic instead of leather. Plastic that's made in plants that leveled animal habitats in order to be built and that cast pollution throughout the environment which will inevitably kill more animals.

Everything in the house seemed to crease and come to a severe point in perfect placement. The bed sheets and comforter, towels, throw rugs, decorative pillows, doilies, all came to a point aligned with some line or corner along the wall or floor. The tablecloth, place mats, and napkins, too, were all placed against the edges of the table leaves. The table set for six, and Harley wondered how often Reed had guests over. He swept his fingers over the top of the television expecting lines of dust from the black plastic to turn the tips of his fingers a grayish brown, but nothing.

Reed's bedroom, too, was another template of perfection except for the closet, which had a paddle lock affixed to it. Harley lifted the lock with the tips of his fingers as if he were lifting a piece of fabric from a stab wound, then went to the kitchen and rummaged through the drawers.

He went back to the lock with a Phillips head screwdriver. He pulled the door open as much as the bracket would allow and it was enough to fit the screwdriver partly into the screw. He turned it, but the angle he was forced to hold the screwdriver caused it to slip. Harley alternated on the screws he loosened. Halfway through his efforts, when he began to realize how difficult it was going to be to put the screws back in, he wondered why he was so curious to know what was behind the door. Outside, the neighbor's sprinkler rattled the chain-link fence and the panic of Reed discovering him forced Harley to push the screws back in. Sweat began to run down the sides of Harley's face and neck. Each time the driver slipped from the screw, he cursed quietly. By the time he finished, the heads of the screws were damaged, but not quite stripped. Harley hoped Reed wouldn't notice.

Harley left the house and made his way back up to the loft. He sat on the top of the steps and calmed himself. The color of the grass and the leaves shifted hues as he allowed his eyes to lose focus as he tried to imagine what Reed was hiding in the closet. Later that night, he sat near the soft glow of candlelight in the loft. He heard a sizzle in the wax of the candle. Several moths fluttered near the flame, and one had hit the wax. He continued to watch them, their chaotic flight. Another drifted into the wick and singed, dropping into the wax with the other. More darted around the light, taking a second chance with the flame, but they didn't get scorched. Harley continued to follow the madness of their flight as they moved the flame of the candle then dart away as if they were made of porcelain. He wondered why they would hover so close to the flame, so close to that violent end.

THIRTY-THREE

Maggie stroked groceries across the scanner. The woman buying them flipped through her coupons, placing the ones she could use on the small shelf above the conveyor belt. The beeping drone of groceries sliding down to the bagger put Maggie in a trance and she spent the rest of the afternoon in a daze—the repetition of her work from year after year allowing her to function like a long drive with a mind full of distraction.

The bar she went to after work had changed, but Maggie barely noticed. They'd repainted the back wall and replaced a few of the broken tables. She sat at the center of the bar where they'd put in a videogame machine that beeped and dinged much like the scanner at her job and perhaps the reason it kept her blank and preoccupied with the emptiness of her thoughts. She'd ordered a club soda with three limes and ignored the bartender when he asked if she'd like him to play some music.

When more people arrived, Maggie began to shift from her trance into more lucid thoughts. Sean's words fed her anger and it grew slowly as she thought more about what else was growing inside her. Other conversations took over the silence. The barstools were different, cheaper, and there was no footrest at the base of them to rest her heels. The surface of the bar was smooth and wasn't as sticky as she'd remembered, nor was there any duct tape over the edge where nails would sometimes snag a thread from her clothing like a desperate friend begging for her to stay or take them with her. There was more light in the corners where men had groped her, too impatient to get out to the car or back to her place.

Maggie, for no other reason but nostalgia, tried to remember the men she'd brought out of there—drunken stumbles through some quest for control of the thing that had happened to her. Most of those mornings after she'd stumble from the bed to the bathroom to vomit. Sometimes, she'd find Harley sleeping in the small space between the end of the tub and the wall where she threw the dirty laundry.

She finished her club soda and ordered another. As she shuffled through her memories of the bar, she began to feel more and more out of place. The place that she remembered was gone. There were new wall hangings, televisions, signs on the bathroom doors designating sex, and some long-standing holes in the walls patched with sheetrock instead of wood or cement. Among all of it, the changes and the peculiarity of being among the new setting, the smell was the same. The same dank, wet odor of wine that had turned was plush in the air and it made Maggie understanding that the room she was in was working on its second chance.

When she finished her drink, she ordered a glass of red wine. She'd never drank wine, but had heard somewhere, probably a conversation in one of her lines at the store, that it was okay to drink when pregnant if it was red wine.

"What kind would you like?"

"Whatever's cheap," Maggie answered.

The bartender grabbed a glass from the sideboard and pulled a screw-top bottle from a shelf below the bar. He smelled the end of the bottle before pouring it into the glass.

"Rough day?"

Maggie turned in the direction of the voice, a man who'd slipped into the barstool next to her.

"Not really, why?" she asked.

The man fiddled with the stirrer in his dark cocktail. His

clothes were blotched with paint, and Maggie wondered why painters wore white pants in the first place, that it would make more sense for them to wear the color pants that they were painting with.

"Just wondering," he mumbled under his ball cap, which was also spotted with paint. "I usually don't see girls like you in here this early unless they've had a rough day."

"I see. What kind of girl do you think I am?"

He scratched the thin beard on the side of his face. The ends of his fingers were like small plums, round and misshaped compared to the thinness of his fingers. He glared at her over the top of his plastic-framed glasses. "You look like the kind of girl who has a lot going for her, too much to sit in this shithole in the afternoon waiting for some townie to hit on her. It's either that or you just broke up with your boyfriend, in which case you're waiting for someone to hit on you."

"Why does that mean I'm waiting for someone to hit on me?"

"You're a woman." He chuckled to himself and took a drink.

"That's interesting. So what makes you think I just broke up with my boyfriend?"

"Other than the fact that you just said so? Honey, if you had a boyfriend worth a shit, he wouldn't let you come in here without him. Besides, probably a dumb son of a bitch anyway to let someone like you go."

Maggie tried to camouflage her discomfort with a gulp of wine. The wine was sweet initially, but the taste went bitter after she swallowed, and her tongue felt as though it'd been blotted with a paper towel. She swabbed the sides of her mouth to regain moisture. When she looked down, she noticed the man's sneakers didn't have laces.

"Did you have a rough day? It looks like someone stole your shoelaces." Her words came out jagged and nervous.

The man sipped his drink. "I work barefoot. It's easier to slip 'em on and off this way. And since you asked, every day I'm alive is rough on somebody but me. I'm living the dream."

"And what dream is that?"

"Right now, that's more of a fantasy."

"Fantasy?"

"Yeah."

"Of?"

"How rough I'd like to be with you."

The man smirked and looked at her through the corner of his eye. When he took another drink, Maggie slid an inch away from him on the seat of her stool. Sickness rose in her stomach and her hands trembled. The man looked down at her hands when she pressed them flat against the bar.

"No reason to be nervous," the man said. "Or pretend like you're not sitting in here waiting for some cock."

Maggie's hands stopped shaking. She turned her head slowly. "What did you just say to me?"

The man parted his lips and Maggie smiled. She leaned toward him. "If you make me wait any longer, I'm going to find another place to go."

The man choked down a dry swallow. It was easy for them to speak of things they couldn't do, men, but they had a difficult time taking that first gulp of humility when they were asked to back up the things that they claimed. They'd offered her everything. She'd heard everything and forgotten some of the promises, and some of the promises they sent to her were sealed with even more promises. Love, especially, but that never came, never washed up on shore. That bottle sank in the ocean somewhere or it broke and that letter dissolved into silt on the sea floor.

Maggie leaned back and watched the man's eyes circle for a decision.

"What's wrong?" Maggie asked.

"Nothing," the man said. "Where is it you want to go?"

"That depends. I was hoping to get some cock hard enough to fuck me through the back seat into the trunk."

The man swallowed again.

"Don't you think I should know your name or something?"

"I'm here for cock, remember?"

He took another drink. "Are you serious?"

Maggie sighed. "I guess you're just one of those guys who likes to talk big. Time for me to go."

"Hold on. I'm coming."

Maggie left her drink at the bar. She focused on not biting through her own lip as she strutted toward the door. The man followed, a few steps behind her, into the dirt parking lot. Maggie unlocked the driver's side door then reached through to unlock the back. The man's hands slid down her ass over and between her legs where his big-tipped fingers dug into her crotch like he was pushing food remnants through a sink drain. Maggie felt the skin on her lip break, tasted the small drops of blood that formed.

She slid over in the back seat allowing the man room. He reached for her tits as he shut the door and Maggie pushed his hand away.

"Lose the clothes," she said.

The man breathed through his mouth. She watched intently, unblinking while the man slipped off his shoes and his shirt. He pushed his pants to his ankles. Maggie slipped her hand into his boxers and gripped his cock—a thin, rigid appendage that failed to cover even half of her hand. She fought her urge to pinch the tip of it and pushed his boxers down, carefully pulling those and his pants over his ankles.

"You gonna suck it?" he asked.

Maggie straddled him and pushed his burrowing face from her tits. "Yeah. But I changed my mind about the back seat. I want you in front." She rolled from him toward the door they'd entered, forcing him to move across the seat. She reached over and unlocked the other door. "Get in front."

"What? I'm naked."

"Nobody's going to see. Hurry up."

The man looked through the windows then slipped from the back seat and Maggie locked the door as she closed it.

"What the fuck are you doing?"

She sprawled toward the other doors and locked those. The man slapped the hood of the car and punched the window.

"Bitch, what the fuck are you doing?"

She rolled over the front seat of her car and started it. The few people who were standing outside the bar smoking pointed toward him.

"This isn't fucking funny. Open the fucking door, cunt."

Maggie slipped the car in reverse and backed up. The man pounded on the hood and stood in front of the vehicle when she backed out of her space. The other patrons filtered from the bar to watch, holding their drinks and pointing. The man covered his genitals with one hand and swore and pounded on Maggie's car as she rolled through the parking lot.

THIRTY-FOUR

Harley walked around the hospital parking area until the heels of his feet felt bruised and fragile. He walked down the rows of bumpers searching for his car, hoping that he would find a way to get it to start. Sunlight glinted off the rear windows and hurt his eyes. He waited until he'd covered the parking lot multiple times before he went inside to ask about the vehicle.

The woman at the desk was leaning over it, jotting down notes on paper inside of a manila envelope. Harley smelled Italian salad dressing and noticed that the woman was chewing. She swallowed quickly as he approached.

"Yes, can I help you?" she asked and tongued a piece of lettuce from her upper gums.

"I came in a while ago and I had a concussion. My friend parked my car and I can't find it."

"Did your friend tell you where it was parked?"

"No, but I've searched the entire parking lot."

"It may have been towed."

"Why would it be towed?"

"Well, if you didn't have a parking pass or it was parked in a handicap spot, sometimes they tow."

"Do you have any idea who could have towed it?"

"All of our towing is done by A&A Wreckers. You should call them. They'll be able to tell you where your vehicle is. Sir, when did you say you checked in?"

"I don't really remember the exact date."

"Well, I'm a little surprised you waited to retrieve your vehicle."

"You must not answer many phones around here."

"Why? Did you call?"

"No. Lady, you're obviously deaf. I just told you I came in here with a concussion. How was I supposed to drive my car?"

"Well, were you mute?"

"No."

"Then you could have called before your car was towed. Now if you'll excuse me there are people with illnesses that take priority over your negligence."

"You could never be on a tampon commercial."

Her face twisted with confusion and he walked out of the hospital. Harley stopped at a payphone, but the page that would have had A&A Wreckers was torn from the white pages and there were no yellow pages aside from the sliver left in the spine from where they were once attached. He sulked over the path home where Emily had held his hand and led him. Dogs suffered in the noise of their own barking behind windows he couldn't see in. He could only hear the scrape of their claws against the glass, then the faint rumble of their surge to another window.

The day had grown hotter in the few hours Harley had wandered down to the hospital and back. Reed had him in the backyard minutes after he returned cutting brush that was creeping over the lawn. The sun burned against his shoulders and strands of bushes tapped his arms with their thorns as he chopped them at the base.

Reed came into the backyard with a bottle of water. Harley took it and chugged down a few gulps.

"You doing okay?"

"Yeah. I'm fine."

"I haven't seen Emily around that much. Are you two not seeing each other anymore?"

"I've been busy."

"Well, like I said before. You don't need that kind of thing in your life."

Reed walked back to the house and Harley thought as his sweat entered the scrapes on his arms and stung. He thought back to how Emily had pushed his hand from hers. Things were simpler when he didn't have to care what people thought of him—when he could ignore them. He had been content with the fact that people thought he was a freak.

After another hour, Reed came back out to the lawn where Harley worked. He carried a bottle of beer and a towel. Harley dropped the shovel he was using to dig out the roots of the bushes he'd cut.

"You're looking a little parched," Reed said, dangling the towel in front of Harley. "At least you're getting some sun. Beer?" Reed held out the bottle.

Harley took it and brought it to his lips. He waited for Reed's approval, as if him handing Harley the beer hadn't been enough. When Reed nodded, Harley took a sip. It was cold and the flavor was crisp as it washed over his teeth and took the stickiness from the inside of his mouth.

"Good stuff?"

Harley squeezed a burp into silence between his lips. "Yeah. It's great."

"Excellent. I have a five more in the fridge for you. Maybe when you get this done you can come in for a shower and we'll watch a movie or something. God knows, if it doesn't rain soon everything's going to turn to dust."

Harley shrugged, too delighted with the taste of his beer to focus on more work. "Okay," he said.

Harley stared at the bottle. He held the mouth of it close to his nose and smelled the sickly sweet aroma, almost like sweat. He took an aggressive swig forcing the beer to foam and spill out over the neck of the bottle. Harley licked it off his knuckles and the bottle.

"Easy now," Reed told him and chuckled to himself.

Reed draped the towel over Harley's shoulder and went back inside. Harley watched the foam in the beer settle. The beer was warmer when Harley took his next drink, and he didn't like it as much, but finished it with enthusiasm anyway. He left the bottle on the ground and went back to his digging. The ground was bored with small round holes when he finished. Clumps of dirt rested on the grass and Harley worked a few of the bigger ones into the ground with his boot. He took a few moments to admire his work, the damage. A pile of thorn bushes and their butchered root systems lay drying in a heap beneath the pressing sunlight. Harley jabbed the shovel into the earth and picked up the empty bottle. He wiped the sweat from his eyes with the towel and went inside.

The moaning came from the living room. The sound of it was familiar, like the whimpers he heard in the boys' home. A flash of concern slowed Harley as he moved through the house. As he rounded the corner into Reed's living room, a split-second before he saw that the moans were coming from the television, Harley recognized the familiarity of those sounds. He'd heard them slipping from Maggie's room time and again. On Reed's television, a woman was bent over a table, her torso stretched across it and her fingers gripping the sides of the wood while a tanned and muscular man whose body hair had been shaved thrust into her from behind. The woman was sweaty. Her blond hair clung to her face and it seemed as if the moment Harley noticed it, the man fucking her lifted his palm over his head then slapped the woman's ass.

Reed looked up at Harley from the couch. "Come have a beer and check this out with me."

Harley beckoned his legs and feet to move, anything, but he stood there motionless and gawking at the space in the room between Reed and the television.

"Come on, Harley. Don't be shy. It's just a couple people fucking. Haven't you ever seen porn?"

Harley had seen women in his magazines and occasionally

his mother doing things he'd seen in those magazines, but he'd never watched a video. He wondered if all those boys who were such good friends in high school had watched the pornos they talked about seeing together. The woman in the video spit on the man's balls and stroked him.

"Guy's got a big dick, hunh?" Reed said.

Harley tried to determine what was most shocking.

"Harley, Jesus Christ, sit down. You're acting weird."

Harley found movement but the shock was still there. His body felt like numbed gums as he shifted toward the couch and sat near the armrest farthest from Reed. Reed pulled a beer from the bucket on the coffee table and handed it to Harley. Harley twisted the top and took a sip, hoping it would comfort him in some way, but it suddenly tasted like piss.

"That chick's pretty hot, isn't she?" Reed asked.

Harley nodded.

"You ever had a girl do that to you?"

Harley took another sip of his beer so he didn't have to answer.

Reed rubbed the inside of his leg. "My ex never did that, and definitely not that well."

"You're not having a beer?" Harley asked.

"Nah." Reed adjusted himself again. "You know, I heard that guys suck the best dick."

Harley took another drink of his beer and felt Reed's stare dump over him like hot grease.

"What do you think?"

"I don't know."

"I bet they do. It makes sense. They know what they like. Why are you drinking so slow?"

Harley gave Reed an awkward smile. "Just trying to enjoy it."

"Don't worry about that. If we run out, I'll go grab you some more."

"I think I'm good."

Harley was uncomfortable. He wondered where he was

supposed to learn how to communicate that. Something a father was supposed to teach you? Harley wanted to know what Maggie would say or do if she walked into the room, but she wouldn't. Shivers forced him to flex the muscles in his legs. He could feel his jaw attempting to quiver but he cushioned his teeth with his tongue to keep them from chattering. His heart raced and it was all he could hear over the gagging and spitting and moaning that came from the television. He wanted to know what people called how he felt. He wanted to know, *scared*.

Reed fast forwarded to the next scene where a tiny blonde slapped two black men's cocks on either side of her face. Harley thought about his last day in the boys' home and he felt the urge to drop his beer and run.

"Now those are some big dicks." Reed muttered.

Harley let his vision blur. The scene didn't excite him. He wondered if it was because Reed continued to stare at him. Reed stood to adjust his pants and when he sat, he sat a few inches closer to Harley and threw his arm along the backrest.

"How big is your dick?" Reed asked. His voice had changed, gone deeper, slowed. "Is it as big as those guys'?"

Harley shrugged. "I dunno."

"You've never measured it?"

Harley shook his head.

"That's crazy. I'll go get a ruler...Or do you need a yard stick?"

"Mr. Reed, I—"

"Oh, don't be a pansy. Every guy measures his dick. Besides, it's me, Harley. I'm not going to tell anyone."

Reed walked out into the kitchen and shuffled through a drawer. Harley's beer had gone warm in the short time he'd had it opened and he spit the mouthful he'd just taken back into the bottle. The ruler was yellow plastic. Reed pinched it with two fingers and tapped it against his other palm. He held it out to Harley and rested his other hand against his hip, a posture that Harley remembered from school when he asked a student to write something on the board.

"I'm all set."

"All set?" Reed stepped forward and dropped on the couch next to Harley, throwing an arm around his shoulders. "Come on, Harley. It's just us. Don't you want to know how big your dick is?"

"It doesn't really matter to me."

"Oh. I get it. You're shy."

Harley tensed, the most rigid he'd ever felt.

"I could help you if you want." Reed's changed voice came back, swarmed around Harley's ear, and Harley turned toward him.

"What do you mean?"

"Well," Reed whispered and looked down toward Harley's knees. His hand slid up his leg and he palmed Harley's crotch. "Like this. I can already tell you're huge."

Harley pushed Reed's hand away with the bottle. "I think I should—"

"You should sit right here and let me take care of this."

Reed moved his hand back to Harley's groin. His other hand gripped the back of Harley's neck and Harley was surprised by his strength. He pushed against Reed, but his grip only tightened. He felt bound, tied, and trapped in a small dark space. The feeling of panic shook through him and chilled his body into shivers. As if trying to snap his imaginary restraints, Harley lunged forward toward the floor swinging his arm toward the back of his neck and felt his elbow connect. Reed slumped back on the couch and fell to his knees on the carpet.

"Jesus fucking Christ, Harley. I think you chipped my tooth."

Harley stood and faced Reed. He moved his hands from his mouth revealing the blood trickling down over his lips. Harley turned and went out and up into the loft.

He stood at the top of the stairs for a long time peering around the space and rubbing away the tenseness in his neck from Reed's grip. He'd fled from Maggie's to find some sort of peace there, a place away from his turmoil of her refusal to love him, and he knew that he had no place to go but back there. Reed came out of the house and looked up at him, where Harley stood. His car keys shook in his hand.

"I don't think this is going to work out, Harley. Probably best if you're not here when I get back."

THIRTY-FIVE

Maggie thumbed through the contents of the painter's billfold, trying to figure out what to do with it. She sat outside on her porch steps and pulled pictures from the worn pockets of the leather, crinkled like a convenience store receipt for a soda and a candy bar. There were slips of paper and discount cards for various local stores, a concert ticket from three years before for a band that Maggie had never heard of. He carried receipts from hardware stores and a small stack of business cards that proved he was a painter by trade. His license matched the name on the cards and Maggie wondered if he were still scrambling around the parking lot cursing her.

The man had seven hundred dollars in cash in his pants pockets, and Maggie counted it twice. It was a little more than she made in a week. She collected his things from the back of the car and stuffed them into a plastic grocery bag. His shoes she dropped on top of the bag in the trash can on the porch and sat down to smoke a cigarette.

Sirens screamed in the distance and grew louder. She heard the slowing of vehicle engines and the sporadic, screaming pulse of the sirens until they'd come to gather on the street in front of her house. Her heart raced. How did the cops know where to find her? The sirens stopped and she listened to the heavy, marching footsteps shuffle down the neighbor's driveway and knock on his door. Relief calmed her, but she retreated inside.

From the edge of her bed, she watched the police through the window. A few moments after they entered the neighbor's apartment, they were leaving with the neighbor in handcuffs. He bowed his head and Maggie forced herself to wonder what he'd done.

She sat in front of the television for most of the night, curing her loneliness and boredom with sitcom reruns and repetitive commercials. There were moments that she found herself dazing, staring off into Harley's room waiting for him to come out and throw some absurd observation in her face. She even missed Sean for brief moments, but they passed when she thought of him and became physically uncomfortable. She took repeated trips to the kitchen to look in the refrigerator as if it would suddenly offer her something she craved.

During one of her trips to the refrigerator, Harley knocked on her door. She grabbed at her chest in panic and turned to see him looking in at her. The knock felt alien to her, and she looked at him like a stranger would then waved him in.

They stood on opposite sides of the kitchen trying to figure out what to say. Harley held a garbage bag full of the things he'd taken when he moved out. Maggie wondered where he'd been after she thought about the length of time he'd spent at the boys' home.

"Where's Sean?"

"Not here." She felt tired suddenly and didn't want to see Harley's reaction when he found out Sean wasn't coming back.

"What's in the bag?"

"My stuff."

"Where ya been?"

"Not here."

Maggie sighed. "What's up?"

Harley had never had to ask Maggie to stay with her. The question, like so many other things he'd been discovering, he didn't have the resources to craft. "I don't have any place to stay anymore. Do you mind if I sleep here for a while?"

"How long is a while? Where's your car, Harley? I didn't

hear you pull in."

"I lost it. It should only be for a couple days. I had to vacate the last place a little unexpectedly."

"What happened?"

"I had a disagreement with the owner about measurements."

"That went over well. You remember where your room is."

"Thank you."

Maggie returned to the couch and Harley followed. He moped into the room and Maggie noticed the blood on his elbow.

"What happened to your arm?"

Harley entered the living room and stood under the light. He twisted his arms to search for what Maggie was talking about until he found a patch of dried blood on the point of his left elbow and rubbed it off on his pants.

"Is that your blood?"

Harley shook his head.

"Whose is it? Is that from your disagreement?"

"Must be. Can I watch TV with you?"

Maggie pulled her feet from the cushions so Harley could sit. Maggie flipped through the channels incessantly, stopping briefly on the channels where an audience laughed and continued through when the laugh was over.

"When's Sean coming back?"

"I thought you wanted to watch TV?"

"You're just surfing."

"He's not coming back."

"You mean for good?"

"Never."

"I'm sorry. It must be painful for you."

"Harley, you don't know what pain is. And where the fuck is my couch cushion?"

THIRTY-SIX

May 1977

When Edith came home, Maggie was still in the bathtub staring at the ripples in the copper colored water where drops fell from the faucet. The water had gone cold long before and her teeth chattered. The pain inside her still shook her legs despite how tightly she pressed them together. Edith called for her, and Maggie looked down at her blue Sunday dress floating in the water. Again, Edith called, a desperation and concern in her voice that trembled Maggie with fear. How could she know? How could she know what had happened already?

Maggie pushed herself from the water and fed her arms through the robe. Edith passed by in the hallway to Maggie's room. Maggie pulled the drain plug and stood in the tub watching the water drop. She had hoped it would have taken the dress with it through the drain. Edith knocked on the door. It was then that Maggie noticed the time. Her mother was home three hours early. She bunched the dress and wrapped it in a towel. From the tub she twisted the knob on the door and opened it.

Edith stood there in tears and Maggie waited for her embrace, to tell her it was okay even though it wasn't. Tell her he'd pay for what he did, but that didn't come. Instead, with a tear sliding over her mother's quivering lip, she said, "There's been an accident. Your brother's dead." The last bit of water slurped down the drain and Maggie felt her gut fold in on itself. Edith's tears spilled more profusely and her arms reached out for Maggie.

That bastard. That heartless fucking all-knowing bastard.

THIRTY-SEVEN

Late Spring 1997

Faggot had been painted across the door of the janitor's closet. The *f* and the *t* were outside the frame of the door on the wall.

"You know who does this?" Bruno asked him.

"No."

"You clean quick. Not a good word."

"Sure, Bruno."

"You see better now?"

"Yeah. A lot better."

"Good. I see nice tush."

Harley was spreading a second coat of paint on the door when Reed and Dr. Ulsin, the principal, came out of the main office. Reed ducked into his room, but the principal walked over to Harley.

"Any idea who did this?" she asked.

"Not a clue."

"There was similar vandalism across the door of a student's house, Emily Jensen." She waited for Harley to speak. "Still no clue?"

"Your guess is as good as mine."

"Harley, Mr. Reed informed us that it was probably Ricky Di'Angelo. He also told us there is a romantic relationship between you and Emily."

"Emily and I are friends. She's busy getting ready to have her baby. There's nothing going on between us."

"Good. It needs to remain that way. We have a strict policy on staff and student relationships."

"I can assure you there is no relationship."

"Alright."

"Can I get back to work, now?"

"Certainly. Thanks for clearing things up for us."

Harley turned to the vandalism and scraped the paint off the tiles on either side of the door with a razor blade while the fresh coat of paint on the door dried. Students milled through the hallway before the first period bell rang. Harley ignored their laughter and how they mumbled *faggot* under their breath in one syllable. Harley finished painting and tagged the wall on either side of the door with wet paint signs. He brought the can of paint back to the storage room.

Harley went through most of the day making little effort to avoid students. He pushed his caddy through the hall in the direction that he wanted to move, bumping and nudging students out of his way. Same with the mop bucket, ignoring students' complaints when he splashed them or scuffed the sides of their new white shoes. The shoes their parents bought for them because they wanted them. Birthday, Christmas, good grades, graduation, no, the only reason they got what they wanted was because they wanted. Harley pushed through their bleating. He mopped over feet in the bathroom stalls when it was time to do the bathrooms and tossed pink toilet deodorizers into the urinals as boys were pissing. But when the bathrooms were empty, he scoured until they were the cleanest he'd ever had them, shimmering and spotless. He cleaned the sink drains and windows, polished the mirrors and stainless steel, organized his closet and bleached the mop. Harley left the school hoping there would be no memory of him there.

THIRTY-EIGHT

Joey sat on the lawn with a small shovel pulling dirt from the ground and dumping it on the sidewalk. Emily leaned against the railing of the steps squinting against the sun. She was wearing a dress and flip-flops. The paint at the end of her toenails was chipped away. Blue tarps had been hung over the graffiti. Joey noticed Harley first and pointed his shovel at him. Emily frowned when she saw Harley coming down the walkway toward her. She pushed herself up and stood.

"Joey, come here."

"Look," Joey said, holding his shovel up to show Harley.

"This is really inappropriate, Harley."

"I don't understand."

"You're always just showing up."

"I thought that we—"

"What? That we had something going?"

"Kind of."

"We don't. I can't do this with you. Especially after…"

"What?"

"After what you said. What you said in the loft. Before you hit your head."

"What did I say?"

"You don't remember?"

"No."

"Maggie. You said Maggie. Actually, it was: Oh, God,

195

Maggie."

Harley's face went hot.

"I didn't really care at first, but then it bothered me a little. And then I found out who Maggie is."

Harley swallowed hard, his insides shaking with a violent tremble.

"I want you to leave, Harley. Joey, come on. We're going inside."

"No, mumma."

"Joey Jensen, you get your butt inside right now."

"So that's it?" Harley asked.

Emily pulled her hair from her bottom lip. "Yeah. That's it."

At first it was a thick, brutal tide of helplessness that swept over Harley as he walked away. The words came at him so effortlessly from Emily's mouth. When he rounded the corner, Ricky's Mustang pulled to a halt ahead of him. Sean climbed from the passenger seat and Ricky had already made it away from the car and stood in front of Harley.

Harley thought of Emily, despite what he knew was going to happen. Her face drifted through his thoughts and he wanted to be near her, like he had been the day they went to yard sales— those days that weren't mired in misery were so few and easy to remember.

"Where are you going, mop-bitch?"

Ricky inched his way behind Harley. Harley remained silent and watched the toes of Sean's sneakers. Ricky smacked the back of Harley's head. "I got expelled because of you."

"So after we beat your ass, are you going to run home and cry in your slut mother's twat?"

Ricky spat on the side of Harley's face. The spray forced his eyes closed. He reached to wipe it off. Ricky started punching.

Harley wanted to hit back against Ricky, but he didn't. He wondered if that was what Maggie meant by pain. The boys laughed as they circled Harley. Harley invited Ricky to hit him again, which he did. His legs grew weaker but he wouldn't go down. For every punch that Ricky landed, Harley reminded himself of every hug, kiss, touch, or praise he'd ever yearned for. His eyes were swelling shut and Ricky finally blasted him in the center of his face. Harley staggered and slipped over the edge of the sidewalk. He went down in the gravel and struggled back to his feet.

"I don't fucking believe this shit," Ricky said.

Harley mumbled something, and Ricky closed in with what remained of his fury, but not enough to challenge the pain that Harley already felt.

THIRTY-NINE

Long after Ricky and Sean had pulled away and the spectators had gone back into their homes, Harley pushed himself from the ground. His arms were heavy and an ache had settled over his entire body as if the pain and damage were too much to suffer in just the places Ricky'd hit him. Pain throbbed through his mouth and he felt his lips and eyes swollen. He tasted the gas and oil from the dirt in his mouth. His back felt bolted to the ground, but he managed to push himself to his knees. As he moved, his body loosened enough to handle the walk, but his face and head throbbed in places and when he reached to check for lumps or blood, the pain would move to a different spot.

While he walked, windows cast light of the half-full moon against the sidewalk, making it a shade of pale white. It was quiet except when he passed the baseball field and crickets chewed the silence of the night away. He thought of his snow globe between his hands imagining the people inside the house screaming to be let out.

Maggie was startled by a knock at the door. The knock annoyed her until she got to the kitchen and saw Harley pressed against the window in the door. His face was warped with lumps and streaks of blood. Some of it had dried into the curves of his ear. When she let him in, she caught his weight as he stumbled forward and guided him to the table where she'd scattered the things he'd had in the bag that he'd left. The snow globe rested at the edge of the table.

"Jesus Christ, Harley. I told you that mouth of yours was going to get you into trouble."

Maggie rinsed a dish rag under cold water and rung it out. She pulled a chair close to Harley and began dabbing the dried blood from his face. When she finished, his face looked a little better. The swelling wasn't as bad as the dried blood made it out to be. His eyes and his cheeks were puffy. Harley lowered his chin and tears began to drip off his face.

"Harley, are you okay?"

"I know what pain is now, Maggie."

She'd seen those eyes before, the way he looked at her. Quivering pulses shot up her hamstrings from the soft part of the back of her knees, spiraled to a whirling at the base of her spine before it coursed through her body and burned in her lips and fingertips. Harley leaned toward her mouth.

"Don't," she said, putting a hand to his chest. "Don't do that. We can't do that."

He moved forward and she felt the softness of his lips against hers. The image of Harley's father flashed in her mind. She felt the curve of the snow globe in her palm. And then she hit him.

FORTY

May 1977

Maggie wedged the thin legs of the chair between her toes as she sat at her vanity. The blue dress she would wear lay spread over the edge of her bed atop a sheet of white tissue paper. The dress had been a gift from her father more than a year before, but she had lacked the female attributes demanded by the dress until then. The roundness had narrowed from her cheeks. Her fingers had thinned, and she combed them through her hair against her ears. She turned her head from side to side to observe her makeup.

She picked up the dress, slipping her middle fingers beneath the seams at the shoulders, and lifted. The fabric felt cool on her neck as she held it over her chest and looked back to her mirror. Changes had sprung through her body over the winter. The T-shirts she'd worn no longer covered the bottom part of her stomach and the men's jeans she liked to wear would no longer button around her hips. She taken on the doting curves of beauty and the dress would finally fit. And she was finally going to be able to wear it to church that day.

The voice of the minister was well forged—broad and deep and essential to the size of the room. He told them what pages to look at, and in unison heads dropped to the pages of their precious books where the answers to all their questions and their source of redemption lay ready for interpretation. Thumbs pressed against the thin paper and the pages fluttered releasing a sound like the whispers of collected prayers falling against the curves of an ear. They found their page, the passage, and their heads moved back to the interpreter. He read to them about Sarah and her unanswered prayers for a child until God finally made her a mother. Then minister's voice died off and Maggie sat oblivious, thinking only of how beautiful her dress was, and thumbed over the lace at the hem.

Church that day had kept her moving more than usual, and Maggie grew impatient in her efforts to keep the dress from wrinkling. Each time before she sat, she pulled the dress taught around the back of her legs to keep it from bunching and wrinkling. When she stood, she smoothed the dress out over her back side, making the fabric form around the plump curve of her ass and the congregation sang: *He is Love.*

At the end of the closing prayer, Maggie's mother sighed the way she did after the closing prayer every Sunday. She toted her bible with one hand and the tension that toed a scowl on her face had lifted. Maggie paid much less attention that day despite the compliments her mother received for having such a darling young lady. Even that had changed. She didn't look like a child anymore.

Maggie rode on the edge of her mother's seat on the way home. The thin rubber tube that trimmed the edge of the bench seat pressed a red line across the back of her ass. She held the dashboard with both hands. Edith hurried them home in their teal green station wagon to change for her overtime hours at the plant—second shift at a plastic textile manufacturer. Maggie took extra care on Sundays not to bother her mother on the way home from church, because Edith hated the fact that she had to work on a Sunday. Her face would bear a tired, defeated look that Maggie hoped she would never have to wear.

When they arrived home, Maggie hovered at the kitchen door stealing glances of her brother's friends Roger and Devon. The three of them sat in the living room. Roger was older than the other two boys, and Maggie had taken note of him before. While the other boys her brother's age had gone soft drinking beer and hanging out in sand pits, Roger had kept himself thin and toned by swimming at the YMCA. He, also unlike the other boys, kept his hair short and shaved. He wore burgundy corduroy bell bottoms and a T-shirt. He didn't wear a belt like the other two boys and the fly of his pants was down a quarter of the way. Maggie felt something happen *down there* as she stared, something magic and soft and grinning.

Roger and Devon sat on either side of a laundry basket filled with linens on the couch. Billy, her brother, sat in the old recliner next to them pawing at his mustache with his thumb. Her mother rushed through the house and passed her in the kitchen. When her mother pulled the car onto the street, Maggie made her way into the living room.

Devon spoke first, glaring at her through his thick, large, rimmed plastic glasses. "Looking good, Maggie," he said and nudged the laundry basket for Roger's attention.

"Yeah, Maggie. Looking good. You ever going to wear something like that to school?"

Maggie blushed. "Maybe."

Devon laughed. "'Maybe,' she says. What classes are you taking?"

"Ugh," Maggie groaned. "The most boring ones." She felt the lie in her voice as her words came out. She loved her classes, but in her want for their attention, she said what she thought they wanted to hear. Her hands began to shake and she felt an embarrassing panic creep into her. She pushed through her shakiness with a question of her own. "Do you guys like your classes?"

"Only when we don't go."

Maggie let out an awkward giggle that left the boys quiet

and trying not to laugh. Her brother belched and reached for another beer in the sack beside the chair he sat in. Maggie gave him a disgusted look.

"Anyone ask you to the prom, Maggie?"

"A couple of boys. I'm not really sure I want to go. With them, I mean. Do you guys have dates yet?"

"Hey Maggie, stop acting like a fucking whore and buzz off," her brother said over the top of his beer can.

Maggie gasped. "You're a real jerk, Billy."

"What's your problem, Billy? We're just asking her how she likes high school."

"She doesn't need to be down here."

Maggie felt a surge in the room as if the distance from the boys had become greater. They became blurry and she realized she was tearing up. She ran past the boys and up the carpeted stairs to her bedroom. The room went dark when she drew the shades, the color of everything fading to silhouette and shadow. The boys' muffled conversation downstairs ended and she parted the shade to watch them pull out of the driveway. When she turned, Billy was in her doorway tapping the bottom of his beer can against his thigh.

"What do you want, Billy?"

"I see how you've been acting."

"Have you seen how you've been acting?"

"We're not talking about me. I've seen the way you look at boys." He moved toward her placing his beer can next to the hairbrush on her vanity.

"Billy get out of my room."

"Why?"

"I want you out of my room, Billy." She backed to her bed and sat forgetting about the wrinkles.

"I don't think you do, Margaret. I think you want me in here."

"Well, I don't. Now please leave."

He took a quick step and gripped her face, mashing her

cheeks against her teeth. The biggest concern she had as she struggled was her dress. Before she realized what Billy was doing, she was facedown on the mattress and Billy's fingers were crawling up her leg under the dress. Her first instinct was to yell for her brother, for him to save her. She wished she'd kept the shades open, wished that God could see into her windows and stop it. The muscles in her shoulder began to stretch and tear. She pushed against his shin with the edge of her foot, kept pushing even after he'd torn the panties from her hip. Then his belt buckle hit the floor by her foot.

"Flaunt your fucking shit around like you're some sort of princess." He spit into his hand and worked his fingers in a circular motion on the spot she was told to protect. The spot she was told to save for marriage. The air felt cool against her bottom forcing a chill around her body. His penis tapped against the top of her thigh like a soft, polite knock. "Here you go, princess."

A second later he was bunching and wrinkling the light blue fabric of her dress into his fists and his thrusting stopped. He fell away. A tussle of ascending pant legs and the chime of his belt buckle. Her torn cotton panties slipped down to her ankles. The back of her knuckles brushed against the lace on the hem of her dress as her arm fell from the small of her back.

FORTY-ONE

Late Spring 1997

Maggie pulled the wet frays of hair from her face in the shower. Her throat tightened while she thought of Harley. She couldn't get his face out of her mind, what he tried to do. She shuffled her hands against her skin which was rubbery from the hard water. She rubbed over her stomach, and her legs grew weak with the image of Billy—of the person who looked so much like him.

The water was going cold and Maggie pinched at her stomach. The days and nights from past years had left her floating through her life, moving arbitrarily down a conveyer belt, stuffed into sacks and consumed. The significance of her need had burrowed through her and came into the light—exposed to the world, a world of finger pointing and hostile whispers.

The water spin down the drain and she turned the valve on the shower and lifted the lever for the stopper on the tub. The water pooled at her feet and she sat, ignoring the shiver of the water rising around her. She adjusted the small mirror clamped to the edge of the tub so she could see her face and curled her wet hair behind her ears with her fingers. What was worse, she decided, as she picked up the razor blade she'd placed in the soap tray, was waiting for something to happen.

Harley woke up on the floor. Blood that had seeped from his mouth was sticky on the linoleum. The snow globe was on its side at the edge of the pool of blood. He tried to remember what happened as he pushed himself up and leaned against the cabinet below the sink. Dizziness. An ache in his jaw as he tried to call out for Maggie. Aside from the kitchen, the only other light on in the apartment was the coming from beneath the bathroom door. He stood and went to the door and knocked.

"Maggie."

He waited for an answer, but Maggie didn't offer one. Harley took a breath and pushed his mind to think of something to say.

"Maggie, I'm sorry. I'm sorry for whatever I did that makes you hate me so much. I just… Why do you hate me, Maggie?"

"Are you going to answer me? Maggie?"

Harley punched the door, jarring it from the latch, and it parted slightly. He could see her hair draped over the edge of the tub, the water crimson. Maggie's eyes were closed. Her face expressionless.

Harley rode in the ambulance with her. The paramedics worked on her, pumping air into her lungs and checking her heartbeat with a stethoscope. One of them spoke into his radio, a summary of her status so the hospital would be prepared when she arrived. They'd asked Harley questions, but he couldn't remember if he'd answered them or not. At one point he looked through the thin rectangular windows on the back door and hoped to see the flames of the world burning behind him.

At the hospital, the medics rushed Maggie into the ER. They left Harley in the hallway shunned and held back by nurses. He made weak attempts to move past them.

"You can't go down there."

"What's happening to her? Where is she going?"

"She'll be going to surgery. You'll have to wait out in the lobby."

The nurses turned and trotted away from him. A hand gripped his arm.

Harley turned to the receptionist.

"I'm going to need you to come with me to answer a few questions."

The woman guided him to the counter in the middle of the waiting area. He stood and waited for her to get to her computer.

"When can I see her?"

"When she gets out of surgery and she's able to have visitors. What is your relationship to her?"

"She's my," Harley hesitated. "She's my mother," he finally stated.

"And your name is?"

Harley answered her, and the subsequent questions she asked him.

When the receptionist asked him for his identification to verify the submission report that she'd been filling out, Harley looked at her dumbfounded.

"Why do I need identification?"

"We have to file this report with the police."

"Why?"

"It's policy."

"I don't have my ID."

The woman folded her hands in front of her.

"You're lying to me," he told her. "Why would I need an ID?"

"It's policy, I told you. You won't be able to see her unless you provide identification. Her visitation will be with family only and you're not listed as one of her contacts."

"This is fucking bullshit."

"I understand your frustration, but it's hospital policy in events like this."

Tears welled in his eyes. "Why are you doing this?"

"Mr. Remick, I'm sorry, but—"

Harley turned and fled the hospital.

An ache stabbed at his shoulders while he ran, mile after mile, darting through intersections and through parking lots. He ran over the manicured lawns and flower beds and over the crumbling sidewalks, leapt over fences and garbage cans and bicycle racks. He tore through bushes and small groups walking down the sidewalk. When he got to Maggie's, he threw up on the sidewalk.

FORTY-TWO

Maggie tried to pull on the edge of her sheet to move the cover over her chest but her fingers wilted in response to the stubborn pain in her wrists. She slipped her hands below the sheet and pushed it up with her forearms and slithered her shoulders down the bed until she could lower the sheet down to her neck. She'd cut deep, pressing the back of the blade with her index finger for her first wrist. The blood had run slick over the blade after the first cut and made the next cuts easier. Her fingers had twitched and dropped into a mannequin stillness. She made the cuts in her other wrists biting the blade and dragging her right wrist over her cheek like a cat pawing its face clean, leaving the streak of her blood over the line of her jaw. She'd smelled dirt, rich earthy soil, and sank into the warm water womb of the tub.

A nurse knocked on the door and Maggie looked over at her. "Ms. Remick, you have a visitor."

Maggie squeezed her eyes shut. She was weak and even that seemed to drain her beyond recovery. She didn't want to see Harley and her thoughts of him made her wonder how she'd gotten to the hospital.

Edith stepped into the room, stepped past the nurse, and sat in the cushioned wooden chair against the wall.

"How are you feeling, Margaret?"

"I'm not really sure yet. How are you feeling, Mother?"

Her mother adjusted her hands. "I've prayed for you."

"Oh, Jesus. Here we go."

Edith placed her purse next to the chair. She pulled a leather-bound Bible from the purse and unzipped the cover. "I want to read you something."

"I don't want to hear it."

Edith pulled on a satin place marker and the thin pages of the book folded over. "He that dwelleth in the secret place of the most High shall abide under the shadow of the almighty."

"Stop, Mother."

"I will say of the Lord, He is my refuge and my fortress: my God; in him I trust."

A doctor stopped at her door and pulled her charts from the slot outside. "Okay, Ms. Remick." She stopped, noticing Maggie's mother in the chair. "I apologize. I hope I'm not interrupting."

Edith glared at her. "I'm reading my daughter the scripture until the doctor arrives, so if you don't mind…"

"I am the doctor, and this will only take a minute. Your scripture will be there when I'm finished."

Edith folded her hands over the pages and looked at the doctor with disdain.

"How are you feeling, Maggie?"

"Like I need a hot bath."

"Well, that's going to have to wait a few more days. I don't want you getting your stitches wet. You're a lucky girl. You lost a lot of blood, but you'll be fine, and the baby, too."

Maggie turned her head to the window and whimpered.

"The baby?" Edith asked.

The doctor, pulling her stethoscope halfway over her head, let it fall back into place. "I'll come back in a moment. You need rest, Maggie."

"You're pregnant?"

The doctor looked at Edith. "She needs complete calm. I don't want her heart rate increasing."

* * *

Harley wandered down the corridor toward Maggie's room. A doctor left the room and the stern voice of another woman snapped in the air. He inched closer to the door and leaned against the wall.

"Who's the father?" the woman asked.

"I don't want to do this, Mother."

Maggie's voice was weak and trying.

"Suicide is a sin and in the eyes of God you've compounded that sin by risking the life of the unborn."

"Well the eyes of God seem to be pretty busy. I'm glad he has you on the lookout for sin."

"Margaret. Why do you speak to me this way?"

"Because I don't want to hear your bullshit about Jesus or God or sinning."

"You need to be saved."

"I needed to be saved a long time ago. You were there. You should know."

"Why do you make me feel like I lost both of my children?"

"Do not bring him into this. Don't even say his fucking name."

The woman allowed a faint smile of revelation slip across her mouth. "It's all clear to me now. You were jealous that I grieved for your brother."

"No, Mother. I wasn't jealous. I was pissed he didn't die the day before."

"You say horrible things, Margaret."

"So do you, Mother, and you use God to justify them."

"I speak truth."

"You speak shit. You knew what happened to me, and you still made me go through with it."

Harley would have laughed had he not been shocked by hearing Maggie lash out so effectively against her mother. He peeked around the corner to see.

"You got yourself into that position, Margaret. I wasn't going to allow you to bring more sin into my house."

"The sin was already in your house. All you did was bring more into it."

"That's not true."

"It is true. You and your precious son. I hope he's burning in hell."

The woman stood up. "How dare you speak of him that way?"

"How dare you stand there and tell me what a precious gem he was? Why do you think Harley looks so much like him?"

The woman wilted. Her eyes darted back and forth over the square tiles on the floor. Harley stood in the hallway trying to make sense of what Maggie was saying, and as if she knew he needed more clarification, Maggie continued.

"That bastard fucked me in my Sunday dress in your home and you made me have his child."

"You lie. You wouldn't let…"

Margaret sat up in the bed. Blood bloomed to the surface of the bandages on her wrists. She spoke through her teeth, almost snarling. "I didn't *let* him."

The woman shook her head. Maggie's machine began to beep. Her eyes rolled behind her eyelids and she fell into the mattress. Doctors and nurses rushed down the corridor. Harley stared blankly at the wall across from him. Maggie's mother was shooed from the room and she stepped into his line of vision. Her mouth began to move, mumbling for Jesus until her head snapped toward him. He locked his eyes into hers as she gaped, her eyes filling with tears.

She whispered, *Billy.*

Harley walked down the corridor away from her and out of the hospital.

FORTY-THREE

The edge of the pavement curved downward where Harley stood to meet the hot ridge of the rain gutter embedded in the sidewalk. Cars veered closer to the yellow line slowing as they passed him with dirty looks of his invasion of their driving path. The wind trailing them blew into his shirt as the sun wiped layers of heat on his skin. He stared blankly at the children riding their tricycles in circles at the top of the driveway across the street. The red flag of the mailbox of their house stood erect and the guttural thump of a big rig engine fighting gravity made its way closer. Ten yards to Harley's right, the speed limit sign said fifty-five, and he twisted the toe of his shoes in the bits of sand at the edge of the street. A shimmering bumper pushed against the light reflecting against it, the chrome bolts of the wheels spinning with the tires in a blur of dizziness he wanted to end. The truck didn't veer toward the line like the other cars. Harley squeezed the edge of the Zippo into the knuckle of his fingers until it felt like the overzealous bite of a playful dog. The truck passed and the wind it carried slipped into his sleeves pulling him. Harley stepped backward onto the sidewalk and wondered if he would have been able to taste the chrome and dead bugs and dirt smeared over the metal or smell the brake dust when it tried to stop.

Harley remembered the sight of her, the heavy weight of her body as he pulled it from the tub. She wanted to die because of what happened to her, because he happened to her. He pulled the lighter from his pocket and snapped a flame into the air. He touched the flame to a string stretching from the bottom button of his shirt and watched it coil and blacken and disappear. He thought of the fire he'd started in the driveway at his mother's apartment—the fire that sent him away and offered Maggie a break from his existence. He'd stood close to the flames, pressing his palms as deep into the heat as he could stand, until he could feel the lingering warmth of them against his thigh when he pressed them into his pant leg. He closed the lighter and turned, bearing the same tight line of the closed Zippo on his lips.

He began to walk through the parking lot, staring at the cracks along the walkways as if his glare would ignite the dandelions struggling to grow there. He wanted to take their place, turn to seed, and become a wish that wouldn't come true. The calm that settled over him was unlike anything he'd ever felt. There was no confusion with what he would do. In his mind, he saw the path he would take as crisp and sharp as the points of a flame. He could taste the ash of everything that had ever hurt Maggie on his tongue. It was a perfect summer for fire.

Edith knelt in her home praying. She frantically looked through her bible trying to find some guidance through the crumbling world around her. Within the pages of her book, she found nothing. The dog-eared pages, the highlighted texts, the notes in the margins, the series of satin place markers or scripture quoted bookmarks were all waypoints to nothing but an enclosing circle of truth—an unraveling of shadow suffocating the light. Her jaw quivered and she looked through the book until her trembling fingers tore the pages she flipped through. Frantic and scared and angry, the woman tore pages from the book and cast them aside. The sound of tearing softened the sound of her wails until the knock came.

Edith did her best to compose herself and opened the door. The man standing before her made her clutch her chest. It was him, the boy she'd lost so long ago. When she reached forward to touch his face, she realized he was soaking wet. The stone-strong line of his jaw pointed toward her and when she looked toward the street for rain, she smelled it. The distinct, stomach-turning smell of gasoline clutched her nostrils. And then she realized that the man standing in front of her was not her son. He stepped forward across the threshold, lifted his arm, and struck the wheel of a Zippo.

The heat forced her to stagger, and in the licking tongues of the flame, she saw the face of her dead son. The fire crawled across the carpet of her home furling the pages of the bible she'd torn. Bible pages blackened, and the flames spread to the corners of the room where they surged up the drapes. This was God's answer for her, a sign for the lack of faith she had. She walked along the edge of the wall to her bedroom. Edith pulled a photo of her son from her nightstand and clutched it to her chest as she lay in the bed. She said nothing, hoped for nothing, and told God she was ready to be received. She lay waiting for the smoke rolling under her door to cradle her and carry her away.

FORTY-FOUR

The fire surged through the house into the upstairs, bursting the windows and showering glass through the streets and yards of her neighbors. Cars pulled to the sides of the road and people got out and watched as the flames lunged and grabbed for the adjacent buildings, seizing them like wrathful fingers around a throat.

Police and fire departments and volunteer firefighters focused their efforts on evacuating homes. The blaze was more than they could handle otherwise. The fire spread and roared into the night drowning out the red flashes of their vehicles. It engulfed the first block within an hour and had spread to the next block up, stopping after it caught the grocery where Maggie worked. The vast parking lot prevented the fire from spreading any further, and the glow reached the darkness outside of Maggie's hospital room window.

Maggie rose from her bed and stood by the window watching a patch of the town burn below her at the bottom of the hill—the part of her world she knew best immersed in fire and shrinking below black smoke. A new strength lifted through her body and she touched her stomach. Harley was down there somewhere, but somehow, she knew that she would never see him again.

Maggie stayed at the window through the night as the fire burned in the darkness and people lined up on the edge of the hospital parking lot hovering in the penumbra between the light from the parking lot and the light of the fire. They brought chairs and coolers and cheered as the flames burned their town, their neighbors' homes. They clapped as the fire took the things from people's lives they'd have to replace with donations and salvage sales. The rooms where they had made love to someone for the first time were gone. The arena that people had suffered and loved and cried and were born and died in burned in the darkness until there was nothing left to burn and dawn arrived to greet the charred landscape.

The air was gray with ash and Maggie's lack of focus. Abruptly, a memory came back to her. She couldn't remember what year it was, which Christmas she bit the tip of her thumb while Harley unwrapped the snow globe from the funny papers she'd used as wrapping paper. But she remembered his face losing color as his eyes followed the white specs sifting through the globe and how he slept with it tucked beneath his arm. Then, she remembered the morning after Christmas when he let his cereal go soggy because he couldn't break his trance from the toy. Maggie readjusted her focus. The ash drifted down outside the window, and she remembered sitting on the floor of Edith's bathroom as the snow fell outside all those years ago when she'd given up on a second chance.

JOE RICKER is a former bartender for Southern literary legends Barry Hannah and Larry Brown. He has also worked as a cab driver, innkeeper, acquisitions specialist, professor, and in the Maine timber industry. He currently lives in Reno, Nevada, and spends much of his free time walking uphill.

JoeRicker.com

DOWN & OUT BOOKS

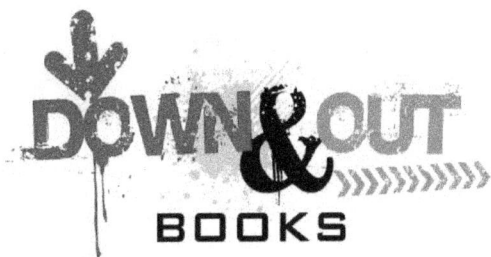

On the following pages are a few
more great titles from the
Down & Out Books publishing family.

For a complete list of books and to
sign up for our newsletter,
go to DownAndOutBooks.com.

ALL DUE RESPECT   SHOTGUN HONEY

Moonlight Rises
A Dick Moonlight PI Thriller
Vincent Zandri

Down & Out Books
March 2021
978-1-64396-189-7

Dick Moonlight is dead for real this time. Thanks to a trio of masked thugs in a dark downtown Albany alley, he's purchased a one-way ticket to the Pearly Gates—that is, until he feels his floating spirit painfully pulled back into his bruised but breathing body. And that's when the real trouble starts.

The Cold War is heating up once again in Vincent Zandri's latest thriller. *Moonlight Rises* is a fast-paced, whip-smart tale of a guy who can't always remember getting into trouble—and can't seem to stay out of it. An unputdownable mystery that's sure to keep you up all night...in a good way.

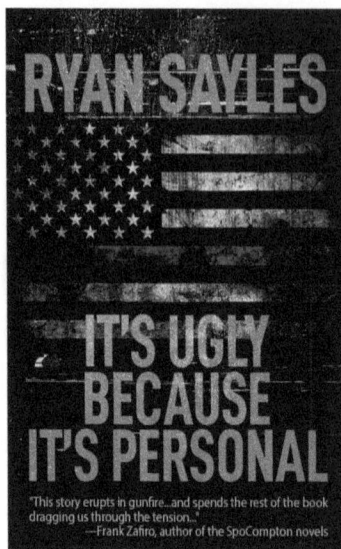

It's Ugly Because It's Personal
Ryan Sayles

Down & Out Books
March 2021
978-1-64396-182-8

In the city of Carcasa, gunshots devastate the night as a patrol officer makes a traffic stop. The occupants—three dealers caught in the act of muling—set into motion a course of actions that can only end badly.

Now, one is dead, another fleeing on foot and the third tearing through neighborhoods in a bumper car-style chase.

Furious, grief-stricken officers are on their heels with their brother fighting for his life on the side of a road.

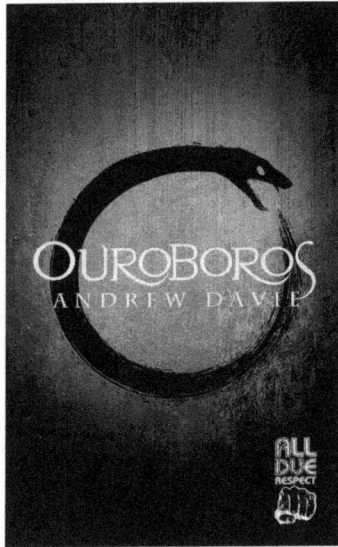

Ouroboros
Andrew Davie

All Due Respect, an imprint of
Down & Out Books
December 2020
978-1-64396-124-8

McGill and Gropper work as unlicensed PIs who operate out of a diner in Charleston, SC. McGill, the face of the operation, is a former police officer. Now incredibly out of shape, he rarely leaves the diner and has a fondness for pancakes, bacon, and coffee. Gropper is well versed in fighting. He doesn't tend to carry standard weapons as he himself is lethal.

McGill and Gropper take almost any job and are willing to break the rules to get these jobs done. As they conduct business, someone from McGill's past returns to enact revenge.

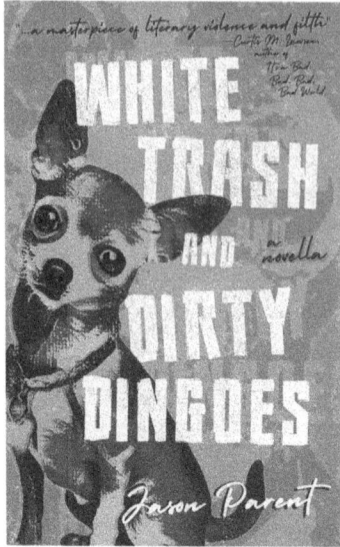

White Trash and Dirty Dingoes
Jason Parent

Shotgun Honey, an imprint of
Down & Out Books
July 2020
978-1-64396-101-9

Gordon thought he'd found the girl of his dreams. But women like Sarah are tough to hang on to.

When she causes the disappearance of a mob boss's priceless Chihuahua, she disappears herself, and the odds Gordon will see his lover again shrivel like nuts in a polar plunge.

With both money and love lost, he's going to have to kill some SOBs to get them back.

www.ingramcontent.com/pod-product-compliance
Lightning Source LLC
Chambersburg PA
CBHW020252030426
42336CB00010B/724